Printed in China

快乐中国——学汉语
Happy China – Learning Chinese

中国中央电视台
《快乐中国——学汉语》栏目组 编

西安

篇

北京语言大学出版社

西安

西安主要景点游览示意图

半坡遗址博物馆

丝绸之路起点群雕

钟楼

碑林

秦俑博物馆

陕西历史博物馆

大雁塔

楼观台

前　言

　　中国的发展令世人瞩目，随之而来的学汉语热潮也在全球兴起。

　　中国中央电视台中文国际频道（CCTV-4）《快乐中国——学汉语》栏目，与中国各地城市以及风景名胜点合作，把饱览名山大川、感受中华民族历史文化与学习汉语结合起来，将汉语言语技能与知识性、趣味性和欣赏性融为一体，创办了独特的寓教于乐的电视教学节目——《快乐中国——学汉语》。

　　通过中央电视台覆盖全球98%的强势传媒，《快乐中国——学汉语》自2004年6月播出以来，引起了海内外观众的热烈反响。不少观众来信来电，希望得到《快乐中国——学汉语》栏目播出节目的文字和音像材料，作为学习汉语的视听说教材。为了满足广大观众的需要，北京语言大学出版社承担了这套文字、声像教材的编辑、出版任务。在此，我们深表感谢！

　　语言是桥梁，电视是桥梁，《快乐中国——学汉语》是沟通你我的桥梁。它把汉语教学搬进大自然的课堂之中，"快乐学汉语，轻松又好记！"此外，我们采用高清晰电视技术和立体声制作的表现手段，并制作成可用于教学的、有多种字幕选择的DVD，充分展示汉语特有的魅力。

　　为了使节目主持人的对话更好地帮助您学说汉语，我们聘请了北京语言大学长期从事对外汉语教学和英语教学的几位教授，对每一集对话进行了加工，增添了生词、注释、替换练习和会话等部分，并负责生词和注释部分的英文翻译。每一集有8~10个生词，有5~8个注释，有模仿练习，也有交际性的活用练习，帮助您更好地理解对话内容，掌握重点词句。

　　为了适应学习者需要，每册收入15集节目（特殊情况除外），并配有相应拍摄点的简介、图片和旅游资讯。由于节目制作还在进行之中，配套图书将陆续出版。

中国中央电视台中文国际频道

《快乐中国——学汉语》栏目组

PREFACE

The development of China has attracted the attention of the world, as a result of which a great upsurge for learning Chinese has been going on throughout the world.

The CCTV-4 program *Happy China—Learning Chinese* offers learners an opportunity to learn the Chinese language and culture while enjoying the beautiful scenic spots in China. Co-operating with the local administrations of the well-known scenic spots, this program well combines the learning of language skills with that of Chinese culture and history in an interesting, informative and enjoyable way.

With a 98% coverage in the world, the program of CCTV was broadcast since June, 2004. Quite a lot of the viewers expressed the hope to have the language materials as a learning aid. In view of this, we have invited Beijing Language and Culture University Press, a leading press in publications on Chinese learning materials for foreigners, to produce and publish these language materials for our viewers.

Apart from the language materials presented in the program, Words and Expressions, Notes, Substitution Drills and Conversations are provided in each book, among which Words and Expressions and Notes are accompanied with brief English translations or explanations. Each book is composed of about 15 episodes of the TV program with brief introductions and photos of corresponding scenic spots and travel guides. As more episodes of *Happy China—Learning Chinese* are coming up, more books will be published accordingly.

CCTV-4

Happy China—Learning Chinese Production Team

西　安

西安市位于中国的西北部，是一座历史悠久的现代化大都市。它地处黄河流域关中平原中部，四季分明，气候温和，除了较寒冷的冬季外，其他时间都比较适合旅游。

西安古称"长安"，是"丝绸之路"的起点。它同希腊的雅典、意大利的罗马、埃及的开罗并称为"世界四大古都"。西安建城已有3100多年的历史。从公元前11世纪开始，先后有周、秦、汉、唐等13个王朝在西安建都，历时1100多年。汉、唐两代更是西安历史上的鼎盛时期，此时的西安是中国政治、经济、文化和对外交流的中心，也是宾客云集的东方大都会。

西安是华夏文明的发源地，拥有大量的历史人文景观。徜徉在千年古都宽阔平坦的街道上，您可以看到历史悠久的西安古城墙，有"石制图书馆"之称的碑林，以及钟楼、鼓楼、大雁塔等西安的标志性建筑；这里还拥有"世界第八大奇迹"——秦始皇兵马俑，中华民族发祥地之一——半坡遗址等中华古代文明的珍贵遗存。因此，许多外国元首都把西安作为访华的必游之地。

丰富的文化遗存使这座生生不息、极富旺盛生命力的城市拥有辉煌的过去，日新月异的现代西安更向世界展示着多姿多彩的今天和未来。完备的城市基础设施，数字化的信息服务功能，拥有100多条国内外航线的西安国际航空港，与以西安为中心的"米"字型高等级公路和铁路网，构成了一个立体交通网络中心；林立的涉外星级酒店，丰富健康的娱乐生活，富丽舒适的旅游购物场所，享誉中外的各种美食，都吸引着众多的国内外游客。

XI'AN

Xi'an, situated in the heartland of the Central Shaanxi Plains in Northwest China, is a modern metropolis with a long history. It has a mild climate with four distinct seasons. All the seasons except cold winter are suitable for sightseeing.

Xi'an was called Chang'an in ancient times. It was the starting point of the world-famous Silk Road. The city is also known as one of the world's four greatest ancient capitals along with Athens of Greece, Rome of Italy and Cairo of Egypt. Xi'an has a history of more than 3, 100 years. Starting in the 11th century BC, a total of 13 Chinese dynasties, including the Zhou, Qin, Han and Tang Dynasties, established their capital city in Xi'an, spanning a period of 1, 100 years. Xi'an had its heyday in the Han and Tang Dynasties, when it became the country's center of politics, economy, culture and international communication, as well as a large metropolis in the East.

As a cradle of Chinese civilization, Xi'an boasts a host of sites of historical and cultural interest. Strolling along the city's broad streets, visitors can see the time-honored city wall, the stele forest, which is billed as the "Library of Stone Books", the Bell Tower, the Drum Tower, the Dayan Pagoda and other landmark historical architectures. In addition, Xi'an is also the location of Emperor Qin Shihuang's terracotta warriors, which is acclaimed as the eighth wonder of the world, and the Banpo Ruins, one of the birthplaces of Chinese civilization. It is no wonder that many foreign heads of states would always put Xi'an on their must-see lists when they visited China.

Xi'an takes pride in its rich cultural heritage and its glorious past. However, this dynamic modern city is more proud of its recent achievements and looks forward towards its prosperous future with confidence. Xi'an has sound infrastructure facilities and digitalized information services. Xi'an International Airport connects with over 100 domestic and foreign destinations. Modern superhighways and railways with Xi'an as center form a three-dimensional traffic network. Luxurious hotels with a variety of recreational amenities, posh shopping malls and savory local delicacies all attract tourists both from home and abroad all year round.

目录
CONTENTS

西安

【第一集】

長樂門

永宁门下

韩　佳：世界上有四座城市，因为它们的历史非常悠久，文化又十分
　　　　灿烂，所以被称为"四大文明古都"。

大　牛：没错。它们是希腊的雅典、意大利的罗马、埃及的开罗，还
　　　　有我们现在所在的这个城市——中国西安。①

韩　佳：西安可以说是一座巨大的历史博物馆，在这里到处都有历史
　　　　的遗迹。您瞧，这就是一处——西安古城墙。

Han Jia: Four cities in the world, due to their extremely long history and splendid culture, are billed as the four greatest ancient cities.

Daniel: Sure. They are Athens of Greece, Rome of Italy, Cairo of Egypt and the city where we're staying, Xi'an of China.

Han Jia: Xi'an may be regarded as a giant history museum. There are traces left by history everywhere here. Look, this is a section of Xi'an's ancient city wall.

大　牛：这里的城墙保护得真不错！

韩　佳：西安的城墙是中国古代城墙中保存最完好的一处，它始建于隋唐，扩建于明代。②

大　牛：明代？

韩　佳：嗯。

大　牛：那应该是六百多年前喽。

韩　佳：嘿，你的历史还学得真不错！

Nǐ lìshǐ xué de zhēn búcuò!
你 历史 学 得 真 不错！

You're quite knowledgable about history!

大　牛：难道西安是隋唐的时候建起来的？

韩　佳：哎，那你就说错了，西安的历史可以上溯到公元前11世纪。早在公元前220年，汉代③的皇帝就开始兴建长安城，把它作为首都，就是今天的西安。哎，大牛，你在听吗？

大　牛：听着呢，听着呢④什么"公元前220年、公元前11世纪"，还有什么"上……上诉打官司"？

韩　佳：哎，我可没有说"上诉打官司"！我说的"上溯"，意思是从现在的时间推算到以前。

大　牛：哦，原来是两个同音词，很容易搞混。韩佳说的"上溯"就是从现在的时间推算到以前。例如：西安的历史可以上溯到公元前11世纪。……

Daniel: The city wall is surely well preserved here.

Han Jia: Xi'an's city wall is the best preserved of its kind in China. The wall was first built in the Sui and Tang Dynasties and expanded in the Ming Dynasty.

Daniel: Oh, the Ming Dynasty.

Han Jia: Yeah.

Daniel: That would be over 600 years ago.

Han Jia: Hey, You're quite knowledgeable about history.

Daniel: Was Xi'an also first built in the Sui and Tang Dynasties?

Han Jia: No, you are wrong. Xi'an's history can be traced back to the 11th century B.C. As early as 220 B.C., the emperor of the Han Dynasty already began to build Chang'an as the capital city, which is Xi'an today. Hey, Daniel, are you listening?

Daniel: Yes, I am. Well... 220 B.C., the 11th century B.C. and er... "shangsu da guansi" (appeal to a higher court in a lawsuit)?

Han Jia: Oh, I didn't say "shangsu da guansi". What I said was "shangsu" , meaning "to trace back in time".

Daniel: Oh, they are two homonyms. People are likely to get mixed up with them. The "shangsu" which Han Jia just said means "to trace back". For example, Xi'an's history can be traced back to the 11th century B.C. "Shangsu" (to trace back or date back to).

大　牛：这座城墙特别长，一眼望不到头。

韩　佳：是啊，西安城墙上吊桥、闸楼、箭楼、垛口，一应俱全。巧
　　　　妙的设计使城墙十分坚固。

Qiǎomiào de shèjì shǐ chéngqiáng shífēn jiāngù.
巧妙　的　设计　使　城墙　十分　坚固。

The ingenious design of the city walls made them incredibly tough.

大　牛：但是从哪里能看出来这里的设计巧妙呢？⑤

韩　佳：你往地上看。

大　牛：啊？这路面怎么一边高一边低？是不是要塌了呀？

韩　佳：放心吧，不会塌的！这路面是故意设计成这样的。

大　牛：这是为什么？人们不怕滑倒吗？

韩　佳：这西安城墙上的石砖路叫"海墁"，一边高一边低是为了方
　　　　便排水，这样城墙就不会被水浸泡坏了。

大　牛：哦，有道理，这个设计不错。那还有其他的吗？

韩　佳：当然有了，我们去看看。

Daniel: This city is especially long. You can't see its end.

Han Jia: Yes. Xi'an's city wall, with its drawbridges, sluice gate towers, ramparts and crenels, is adequately equipped. Due to the ingenious design, the city wall is extremely strong and solid.

Daniel: But from where can we see its ingenious design?

Han Jia: Look at the promenade surface.

Daniel: Why is one side higher than the other? Will it collapse?

Han Jia: Rest assured. It won't collapse. The road surface was designed purposely like this.

Daniel: Why? Weren't people afraid of slipping?

Han Jia: The stone-paved road on Xi'an's city wall is also known as an apron. The sloped road was designed to facilitate the discharge of water. This way, the city wall won't be soaked in water.

Daniel: Yes, quite reasonable. It was a nice design. Are there any other ingenious designs?

Han Jia: Of course there are. Let's go and find them.

城墙上的敌楼附近

韩 佳：大牛，这就是敌楼，守城的士兵可以在上面向敌人射击。

大 牛：这也算不上是巧妙的设计呀。⑥

韩 佳：你听我说完嘛。这些敌楼每座都相隔120米，你知道为什么吗？

大 牛：这还不简单！两座敌楼的距离很近的话，那这样里面的士兵们互相打招呼就很方便了。⑦

韩 佳：错啦！因为古代的弓箭在这个距离之内杀伤力是最强的，两座敌楼相隔不超过120米，敌楼之间就可以起到互相保护的作用了。

大 牛：哎，这个设计倒是挺巧妙的！看来这座城墙是很难被攻破的。

韩 佳：是啊，在冷兵器时代，像这样坚固的城池是易守难攻的，让敌人肯定束手无策。

大 牛："束手无策"的意思是？

韩 佳："束手"是指捆住了手脚，"束手无策"这个成语意思是没有办法了。

大 牛："束手无策"这个成语意思是没有办法了。……

韩 佳：其实不光是城墙本身，还有深深的护城河围绕着城墙，⑧这样就使得城市的防御系统更加完善了。

大 牛：还有护城河呢？我们能去看看吗？

韩 佳：当然可以了，就在那下边，我们可以去那里领略一下古城墙的雄姿。

大 牛：走！

Wǒmen kěyǐ qù nàli lǐnglüè yíxià gǔ chéngqiáng de xióngzī.
我们 可以 去 那里 领略 一下 古 城墙 的 雄姿。

We can go there and take a glimpse of the old city walls.

Han Jia: Daniel, this was a rampart. Soldiers guarding the city would shoot at the enemy from up there.

Daniel: Is this also an ingenious design?

Han Jia: I haven't finished yet. These ramparts are arranged at an interval of 120 meters from each other. You know why?

Daniel: That's simple. Two ramparts were arranged close to each other in order to let soldiers greet each more conveniently.

Han Jia: You are wrong. An ancient arrow shot within this range would be most powerful. At intervals of no more than 120 meters, the adjacent two ramparts were able to protect each other most effectively.

Daniel: It is indeed an ingenious design. It seems the city wall is hard to break through.

Han Jia: Yes. In the times when there was no gunpowder, such a solid city wall would be easy to defend and hard to conquer. The enemy would be "shu shou wu ce".

Daniel: What does "shu shou wu ce" mean?

Han Jia: "Shu shou" means "to bound hands and feet". "Shu shou wu ce" is an idiom, meaning at the end of one's resources.

Daniel: "Shu shou wu ce" is a Chinese idiom which means powerless. ...

Han Jia: In addition to the city wall, there is also a deep moat surrounding the wall. It made the city's defense system even more adequate.

Daniel: There is even a moat here. Can we go and take a look?

Han Jia: Of course we can. It's right down below. We can go there and take a glimpse of the old city wall.

Daniel: Come on.

护城河边

大　牛：真是没想到过了这么多年，这护城河还保存着呢！
韩　佳：我不是跟你说了吗，这西安的古城墙保存得十分完好。
大　牛：你看，还有这么长的城墙！我们不如再多看看吧。⑨

Daniel: I didn't expect that, after so many years, the moat is still kept so well here.

Han Jia: Didn't I tell you that this ancient city wall in Xi'an is best preserved in China?

Daniel: Look, what a long wall it is! We'd better see more of it.

生词　Words and Expressions

1. 悠久　　　（形）　　yōujiǔ　　　long；long-standing；age-old
2. 灿烂　　　（形）　　cànlàn　　　magnificent；brilliant；splendid
3. 遗迹　　　（名）　　yíjì　　　historical remains；traces；vestiges
4. 城墙　　　（名）　　chéngqiáng　city wall
5. 打官司　　　　　　dǎ guānsi　to go to court；to engage in a lawsuit
6. 一应俱全　　　　　yì yīng jù quán　everything needed is there
7. 浸泡　　　（动）　　jìnpào　　　to soak；to immerse
8. 城池　　　（名）　　chéngchí　city wall and moat
9. 领略　　　（动）　　lǐnglüè　　to have a taste of；to appreciate

注释　Notes

1. 还有我们现在所在的这个城市——中国西安。

"所"，助词，用在做定语的动词前，被修饰的名词在意念上是前面动词的受事。

The auxiliary word "所" is used before an attributive verb，and the noun it modifies is the object of the verb it follows in meaning.

例如：我所了解的情况就是这些。

2. 它始建于隋唐，扩建于明代。

"于"，介词，用在动词后面表示时间。

The preposition "于" is used after a verb to denote time.

例如：中华人民共和国成立于 1949 年。

隋唐：即隋代和唐代。隋代（公元 581-618)，杨坚（即隋文帝）所建，都城大兴（今陕西西安）。唐代（公元 618-907）李渊和他的儿子李世民所建，建都长安。

明代：明代（公元 1368-1644)，朱元璋所建，先定都南京，后迁都北京。

Sui-Tang is namely the Sui Dynasty and Tang Dynasty. The Sui Dynasty （581-618)，during which the capital was Daxing （present-day xi'an，Shaanxi Province)，was founded by Yang Jian who was known as Emperor Wendi. The Tang Dynasty （618-907)，during which the capital of China was Chang'an，was founded by Li Yuan and his son Li Shimin.

The Ming Dynasty （1368-1644)，during which the capital was Nanjing，was founded by Zhu Yuanzhang. After his death， his fourth son ascended the throne and made Beijing the capital.

3．汉代

公元前 206 - 公元 220，刘邦所建，都城长安（今陕西西安）。自公元前 206 到公元 25，称为西汉，也叫前汉。公元 25 年刘秀称帝，建都洛阳，自公元 25 年到 220 年，称为东汉，也叫后汉。

The Han Dynasty (206 BC-220 AD)， during which the capital of China was Chang'an (today's Xi'an， Shaanxi Province)， was founded by Liu Bang. From 206 BC to 25 AD, it was called the Western Han and the Former Han as well. In 25 AD， Liu Xiu came to the throne and Luo Yang became the capital of China. From then to 220， it was called the Eastern Han and the Later Han as well.

4．听着呢，听着呢。

"动词 + 着 + 呢"表示动作持续，常用于口语。

The structure "verb+ 着 ＋呢"， a colloquial expression， indicates the continuation of an action.

例如：电视开着呢。

5．但是从哪里能看出来这里的设计巧妙呢？

"出来"是"看"的趋向补语，表示人或事物随动作由隐蔽到显露。

As the complement of direction of "看"，"出来" indicates the process from concealment to revealment of a person or a thing with an action.

例如：这个人我认出来了。

这个谜语我猜出来了。

6．这也算不上是巧妙的设计呀。

"算不上"这里的意思是"不能算作……""不能认为是……"。肯定形式是"算得上"。

"算不上"， the negative form of"算得上"， means "不能算作"or"不能认为是"。

例如：他算不上是艺术家。

7．两座敌楼的距离很近的话，那这样里面的士兵们互相打招呼就很方便了。

"的话"，助词，用在表示假设的句子后面，引起下文。

The auxiliary word "的话" is used after an assumptive clause to introduce the following text.

例如：你有时间的话，可以去看看，那儿的景色太美了。

8. 其实不光是城墙本身，还有深深的护城河围绕着城墙。

"不光"，连词，常跟"而且、并且、还"等搭配，组成递进复句，表示后面的意思更进一层。

The conjunction "不光" often collocates with "而且""并且""还"etc. to form a progressive complex sentence，meaning the latter part of the sentence goes a step further.

例如：我们学校不光有韩国学生，还有日本、泰国等国家的学生。

9. 我们不如再多看看吧。

"不如"，动词，用于比较，表示前面提到的人或事比不上后面所说的。

The verb "不如" is used for comparison, meaning the person or thing mentioned above is no match for the counterpart following it.

例如：今天太热，别去打球了，不如明天再去吧。

替换练习 Substitution Drills

1. 你	历史	学	得真	不错！
	汉语	说		地道
	交谊舞	跳		棒
	京剧	唱		有水平

2. 巧妙	的设计使	城墙	十分	坚固。
精心		宫殿		壮观
科学		卧室		舒适
精巧		手机		实用

3. 我们可以去那里	领略	一下	古城墙	的	雄姿。
	研究		外国建筑		风格
	品尝		西安		小吃
	体验		农村		生活

会话 Conversation

完成下列会话 Complete the following dialogues

（如括号里有词语或提示，请按要求做 Use words or expressions given in the brackets）

A：路面怎么一高一低的？

B：＿＿＿＿＿＿＿＿＿＿＿＿＿＿。（故意）

A：为什么要这样设计？

B：＿＿＿＿＿＿＿＿＿＿＿＿＿＿。

● ●

A：古代人为什么要把城墙修得这样牢固？

B：＿＿＿＿＿＿＿＿＿＿＿＿＿＿。（的话）

A：中国城市中只是西安有城墙，是吗？

B：＿＿＿＿＿＿＿＿＿＿＿＿＿＿。（不光）

西安

【第二集】

韩　佳：哎，大牛，你怎么骑上自行车了呀？

大　牛：在西安古城墙上骑车转上一圈不是很好玩儿吗？

韩　佳：哟，今天大牛的兴致还挺高！

大　牛：那当然了！一边锻炼身体，一边欣赏西安古城，[①] 何乐而不为呢？

韩　佳：好吧，那我们今天就骑着自行车在西安古城墙上好好转转。

　　合：出发喽！走喽！

大　牛：走。

Han Jia: Hey, Daniel, how come you are riding a bike?

Daniel: Isn't it fun to bike around atop Xi'an's ancient city wall?

Han Jia: Oh, Daniel is really in high spirits today.

Daniel: Of course. Keeping fit while enjoying sights in Xi'an, I see no reason why not.

Han Jia: Good idea. So let's both pedal around today and take a nice tour on top of the ancient city wall.

Chorus: Let's set off.

Daniel: Let's go.

城墙上的魁星楼

韩　佳：哎，大牛，停！

大　牛：怎么了？

韩　佳：你看那不是魁星楼吗？

大　牛：是魁星楼啊。

韩　佳：你还记不记得"魁星"是谁呀？

大　牛：当然记得了！"魁星"就是中国古代传说中掌管文章好坏的神灵，人们膜拜他是希望自己能够考试顺利。

韩　佳：没错，在整个西安城墙上只有这座建筑是跟防御丝毫无关的。

Zhǐyǒu zhè zuò jiànzhù gēn fángyù sīháo wúguān.

只有　这　座　建筑　跟　防御　丝毫　无关。

It is the only structure which was not built for defensive purposes.

大　牛：奇怪，为什么要把魁星楼建在这里呢？ 难道是因为这里高，离上天更近吗？

韩　佳：古代人认为在这个位置祭拜魁星效果最好，所以就把魁星楼建在这里了。大牛，你要不要拜拜啊？

大　牛：我呀，还是靠自己的努力，不靠神仙保佑。

韩　佳：说得好！

Han Jia: Daniel, stop.

Daniel: What's up?

Han Jia: Look, is that the Kuixing Tower?

Daniel: Yes, it is the Kuixing Tower.

Han Jia: Do you remember who Kuixing is?

Daniel: Of course, I do. Kuixing is a deity in Chinese mythology in charge of learning. People pay homage to him in the hope of successfully passing an examination.

Han Jia: Exactly. On the city wall, it is the only structure which was not built for defensive purposes.

Daniel: Isn't it strange for ancient people to build the Kuixing Tower on the city wall? Was it because of the height of the wall, which was considered closer to Heaven?

Han Jia: Ancient people believed that a place on top of the wall was the most ideal for worshiping Kuixing. So they built Kuixing Tower here. Daniel, do you also want to pay homage here?

Daniel: I prefer to rely on my own efforts rather than the blessing of gods.

Han Jia: Nicely put.

城墙上

大　牛：能够看到这么大、这么完整的古城墙真是难得！②

韩　佳：宏伟吧？

大　牛：不光是宏伟，看着这城墙，想象一下古代西安是什么样子，那非常有趣啊！那该是多大的一座城市！

韩　佳：我们现在看到的西安城墙它所包括的面积是唐代长安城的七分之一。

大　牛：我们现在来的是"西安"，又不是"长安"。

韩　佳：大牛，这"长安"就是"西安"。明朝之前叫"长安"，从明朝开始就叫"西安"。

大　牛：这么说在唐朝的时候，这座城市还要大，③真是难以想象！

韩　佳：对呀，汉唐时期的长安是世界上最早达到百万人口的城市，文明发达的程度可以跟当时的罗马相媲美。

大　牛："媲美"呀，就是比古罗马还要美？

韩　佳：不是，"媲美"的"媲"是指比得上的意思。④"媲美"是指美好的程度不相上下。

大　牛："媲美"，"媲"读四声，"美"读三声，指美好的程度不相上下。……古长安可以和古罗马相媲美。

Gǔ Cháng'ān kěyǐ gēn gǔ Luómǎ xiāng pìměi.
古 长安 可以 跟 古 罗马 相 媲美。

The ancient city of Chang'an was comparable with the ancient city of Rome.

韩　佳：是啊，要不然怎么说西安是"四大文明古都"之一呢！⑤在历史上长安是一座非常繁华的大都市，到这里来的人可多了。

大　牛：这个我知道，当时有波斯人、罗马人、希腊人……

Daniel: It isn't often to be able to see a huge and well preserved ancient city wall like this.

Han Jia: Is it magnificent?

Daniel: It isn't just magnificent. The wall may help us imagine what ancient Xi'an would look like. That'd be interesting. It must have been a very large city.

Han Jia: The current walled city is only one seventh of the former Chang'an city of the Tang Dynasty.

Daniel: But the city we are in is called Xi'an, not Chang'an.

Han Jia: Daniel, it's the same city. It was called Chang'an before the Ming Dynasty. It's been called Xi'an since the Ming Dynasty.

Daniel: It seems to me during the Tang Dynasty, the city must have been even bigger. It's really hard to imagine.

Han Jia: Yes. During the Han and Tang Dynasties, Chang'an was the world's first city with a population of one million. Its level of civilization was campared favorably with that of Rome.

Daniel: "Pimei" here means even better than Rome?

Han Jia: No. "Pi" in "Pimei" means to be well matched, or rival. "Pimei" also means to be as good as.

Daniel: "Pimei", fourth tone, third tone, means to be comparable with. ... The ancient city of Chang'an was comparable with the ancient city of Rome.

Han Jia: Yes. That's why Xi'an is regarded as one of the world's four greatest ancient cities. In history, Chang'an was once a very prosperous metropolis. Large numbers of people traveled to this city.

Daniel: I know it. They included Persians, Romans and Greeks.

丝绸之路群雕

大　牛：这个外国老人怎么那么面熟。

韩　佳：哦？

大　牛：我知道了，是圣诞老人！

韩　佳：啊，说什么呢大牛？这是阿拉伯人和波斯人，当时他们都是骑着马、牵着骆驼来到西安的。哎，对了，你知道他们来这里干什么吗？

大　牛：这你可难不倒我！早在2100多年前，长安就是丝绸之路的起点，他们不远万里到这里来只有一个目的——贸易。

韩　佳：哎，说对了！当时的长安汇聚了来自各地的特产，⑥同时也吸引了来自世界各地的人。

大　牛：这么说西安是一座十分好客的城市。

韩　佳：嗯，没错。

Xī'ān　shì　yí　zuò　shífēn　hàokè　de　chéngshì.

西安　是　一　座　十分　好客　的　城市。

Xi'an is a hospitable city.

24

Daniel: This old foreigner looks so familiar to me.

Han Jia: Oh?

Daniel: I guess he was a Santa Claus.

Han Jia: What are you talking about, Daniel? They were the Arab and Persian visitors, coming to Xi'an either on horseback or with camels. Oh, yes, do you know why they came here?

Daniel: You can't baffle me with that. As early as 2,100 years ago, Chang'an was already the starting point of the Silk Road. They came from afar only for the purpose of doing trade.

Han Jia: You are right. Chang'an then had products from all over China. It therefore attracted people from all over the world.

Daniel: So Xi'an is a very hospitable city?

Han Jia: Exactly.

入城仪式进行中

嘉　宾：恭请贵宾入城！
大　牛：今天我可是西安的贵宾了！
韩　佳：怎么样，西安很有意思吧？
大　牛：没错！这座繁华的城市，再加上我这个来自英国的朋友，真
　　　　是锦上添花。
韩　佳：瞧，又把他得意上了。

Guest: Distinguished guest, welcome to Xi'an.

Daniel: Today, I am here as a distinguished guest.

Han Jia: Well, is Xi'an interesting?

Daniel: Yes, it is a bustling city. And as a friend from the UK, I have made it even more beautiful.

Han Jia: See how self-assured he is.

生词 Words and Expressions

1. 兴致	（名）	xìngzhì	interest；mood to enjoy
2. 掌管	（动）	zhǎngguǎn	to be in charge of；to administer
3. 膜拜	（动）	móbài	to prostrate oneself in worship；to worship
4. 保佑	（动）	bǎoyòu	to bless
5. 宏伟	（形）	hóngwěi	magnificent；grand
6. 繁华	（形）	fánhuá	flourishing；bustling；busy
7. 骆驼	（名）	luòtuo	camel
8. 不远万里		bù yuǎn wàn lǐ	to make light of traveling a thousand *li*；to take the trouble of traveling a long distance
9. 汇聚	（动）	huìjù	to assemble；to flock together
10. 锦上添花		jǐn shàng tiān huā	to add flowers to the brocade—make what is good even better

注释 Notes

1. 一边锻炼身体，一边欣赏西安古城。

"一边……一边……"，这一结构表示两种动作同时进行，"一边"要在动词前。

The structure "一边……一边……", in which "一边" should be put before a verb, indicates that two actions happen simultaneously.

例如：他们一边喝茶一边聊天。

2. 能够看到这么大、这么完整的古城墙真是难得！

"难得"，形容词，意思是不容易得到或办到，有可贵的意思，也指不常常发生。

The adjective "难得" means "hard to come by" or "rare".

例如：这个机会很难得。

我们俩一个在上海，一个在北京，难得见一面。

3. 这么说在唐朝的时候，这座城市还要大。

"这么说"用于承接前面的话，表示根据前面的情况作出合乎逻辑的推论。

"这么说" is used to continue from what has been said above to indicate that a logical deduction is made based on what has been mentioned above.

例如：这么说你不跟我们一起云南旅游了？

4．"媲美"的"媲"是指比得上的意思。

"比得上"，这是动补结构，表示可以和某事物相比，能达到某事物的水平。否定形式是"比不上"。

The verb-complement structure "比得上", the negative form of which is "比不上", indicates that the subject before it bears comparison with something and comes up to it.

例如：他的英语水平比得上小王。

5．要不然怎么说西安是"四大文明古都"之一呢！

"要不然"，连词，意思是"如果不这样""否则"，引进表示结果或结论的句子。也可以说"不然"或"要不"。

The conjunction "要不然", which can be either "不然" or "要不", means "or else" or "otherwise" and is used to educe a sentence of result or conclusion.

例如：你给他打个电话吧，要不然他会着急的。

"之一"，其中的一个。常与"是"搭配使用。

"之一", meaning "one of", often collocates with "是".

例如：西施是中国古代四大美女之一。

6．当时的长安汇聚了来自各地的特产。

"自"，介词，意思相当于"从"。用在动词后，表示处所的起点。

The preposition "自", equal to "从" in meaning, is used after a verb to indicate the place which somebody or something comes from.

例如：这种茶叶产自福建。

替换练习 Substitution Drills

1. 只有这　　座　　建筑　　跟　　防御　　　丝毫无关。
　　　　　　栋　　楼房　　　　销售
　　　　　　家　　公司　　　　走私
　　　　　　些　　产品　　　　出口

2. 古长安可以跟　　古　　罗马　　相媲美。
　　　　　　　　　　　雅典
　　　　　　　　　　　汴梁
　　　　　　　　　　　燕京

3. 西安　　是一座十分　　好客　　的城市。
　　大连　　　　　　　　干净
　　杭州　　　　　　　　美丽
　　上海　　　　　　　　现代化

会话 Conversation

完成下列会话 Complete the following dialogues
（如括号里有词语或提示，请按要求做 Use words or expressions given in the brackets）

A：我们到外面走走，看看西安的街道怎么样？

B：＿＿＿＿＿＿＿＿＿＿＿＿＿＿＿。（一边……一边……）

A：西安的名胜古迹太多了！

B：＿＿＿＿＿＿＿＿＿＿＿＿＿＿＿。（要不然）

A：听说在唐代当时长安就有很多外国人。

B：＿＿＿＿＿＿＿＿＿＿＿＿＿＿＿。（来自）

A：有不少是留学生吧？

B：＿＿＿＿＿＿＿＿＿＿＿＿＿＿＿。（其中）

西安

【第三集】

秦始皇兵马俑博物馆外

韩　佳：来到西安，有个地方您可不能不去。

大　牛：西安不能不去的地方太多了，不知道你说的是哪个呀？

韩　佳：哎，我先问问你，你知道世界上的"第八大奇迹"吗？

大　牛：知道啊，西安兵马俑。啊？你是说我们今天要去看兵马俑？

韩　佳：对，就是西安兵马俑。

Han Jia: There is a place you must visit when you are in Xi'an.

Daniel: There are too many places that I must see here. Which place do you mean?

Han Jia: Let me ask you first. Do you know what's the eighth wonder of the world?

Daniel: Yes, I do. The Xi'an terra cotta warriors. Oh, you mean we are going to see the Terra Cotta Army today?

Han Jia: Yes, Xi'an terra cotta warriors and horses.

秦始皇兵马俑博物馆一号俑坑展厅内

大　牛：哎呀呀，真是！哎呀呀，真是！

韩　佳：大牛，你别老"哎呀呀"呀，^① 你到底想说什么呀？^②

大　牛：我觉得真是，哎呀呀。

韩　佳：你是不是很吃惊啊？

大　牛：对，小时候我在书上读到过，长大了我在电视上看到过，没想到今天我能够亲眼看见。兵马俑真令人震惊！

韩　佳：兵马俑是中国古老文明的精华，是中国人的骄傲。

Bīngmǎyǒng shì Zhōngguórén de jiāo'ào.
兵马俑　是　中国人　的骄傲。

The Terra Cotta Army is a pride of the Chinese people.

大　牛：哪个民族拥有这样的奇迹都会感到自豪。这里恐怕有几千个兵马俑吧？

韩　佳：这块地方有兵马俑6000个左右，整齐地排列在两个足球场那么大的坑道里。

大　牛：好庞大的一支军队！^③ 制造那么多兵马俑得花多少时间啊？

韩　佳：没有确切的记载。据推算，建秦俑坑花了30多年的时间。

大　牛：真是难以想象这些都是2000多年前制造的。韩佳，这里是全部的兵马俑吗？

韩　佳：当然不是了。在这里发现了三处秦俑坑呢，我们现在看到的只是其中的一处。

大　牛：那我们接着欣赏吧。

Daniel: Yeah, yeah, yeah, oh!

Han Jia: Daniel, what do you mean by yeah? What exactly do you want to say?

Daniel: I feel like yeah, yeah and yeah.

Han Jia: Are you surprised?

Daniel: Right. I read about them when I was a little boy. I watched them on TV later after I grew up. I didn't expect I'd see them with my own eyes today. The Terra Cotta Army is really amazing.

Han Jia: It is part of the cream of Chinese civilization and a pride of the Chinese people.

Daniel: Whichever nation owns this wondrous heritage would feel proud. There may be several thousand terra cotta warriors and horses here.

Han Jia: There are about 6,000 of them here, all lining neatly in a place about the size of two football fields.

Daniel: What a huge army all standing in this large pit! How long would it take to make so many terra cotta statues?

Han Jia: There is no precise record available. According to rough calculations, it took more than 30 years to construct of the pit and the Terra Cotta Army.

Daniel: It's really hard to imagine all these were made some 2,000 years ago. Han Jia, are they the whole of the Terra Cotta Army made then?

Han Jia: Of course not. Altogether, three such pits have been found. The one we see now is just one of them.

Daniel: Let's go on appreciating them.

韩　佳：大牛，你仔细看看，这里有步兵，还有四十多辆战车，它们的阵容庞大、威风凛凛、锐不可当。

大　牛：什么"不可当"？

韩　佳："锐不可当"啊。"锐"是指锐利，"当"是指阻挡，"锐不可当"是指十分凶猛不可阻挡，这个词是用来形容军队的战斗力十分强大。

大　牛：哦，"锐不可当"指十分凶猛不可阻挡。例如：我眼前的这支军队锐不可当。

Wǒ yǎnqián de zhè zhī jūnduì ruì bù kě dāng.
我　眼前　的　这　支　军队　锐　不　可　当。

This army in front of me looks invincible.

韩　佳：你看，它们的排兵布阵就像一部立体的秦代兵书。

大　牛：这军事我可不懂，我是把它们当成一件艺术品来看的。

韩　佳：哦，那你说说你有什么发现。

大　牛：你看，这么多兵马俑都站得整整齐齐的，像是一个模子刻出来的。

韩　佳：哎，这你就说错了，再仔细看看。

大　牛：仔细看还真不一样。有的有胡须，有的没有；长相、发型、穿着都不相同。

韩　佳：这秦俑的一个特点就是一千个人有一千张面孔，人物造型变化多端。

大　牛：我猜这些都是按照真人做成的，要不然怎么会有这么多不同的面孔呢？

韩　佳：这说得还有点道理。

Han Jia: Daniel, look carefully. There is an infantry here, with some 40 chariots. They are all in a huge formidable battle formation, "rui bu ke dang" (irresistible).

Daniel: What "bu ke dang"?

Han Jia: "Rui bu ke dang". "Rui" means sharpness and "dang" means "to stop". "Rui bu ke dang" means "to be very powerful and irresistible". This idiom is used to describe the powerfulness of an army's capabilities.

Daniel: "Rui bu ke dang" means overwhelming or unstoppable. For example, the army in front of me looks invincible.

Han Jia: You may as well consider the battle formation here a 3-D Qin Dynasty book on the art of war.

Daniel: I don't understand warfare. I just regard them as various art objects.

Han Jia: Then tell me what you have discovered.

Daniel: Look, these neatly lined terra cotta warriors seem to be made with a single mould.

Han Jia: Hey, you are wrong. Look carefully again.

Daniel: Looking carefully, I do find they are all different from one another. Some wear beards, and some don't. Their looks, hairstyles and attire are all different.

Han Jia: One significant feature of these Qin terra cotta statues is that they all look different from one another. The images and postures are varied.

Daniel: I guess they were all modeled on real persons, or there wouldn't be so many different images.

Han Jia: That sounds reasonable.

秦始皇兵马俑博物馆的照相厅内

大　牛：走近看才知道，兵马俑的个儿也不矮。

韩　佳：这下知道了吧！这些陶俑平均身高一米八，最高的将近两米，比你大牛还高呢！

大　牛：真是！威武雄壮，令人百看不厌。

韩　佳：是啊，你看他们手上的骨骼和指甲都制作得那么精细。

大　牛：而且整个身体的比例十分匀称，就像真的士兵一样。④

韩　佳：秦兵马俑是非常写实的。简洁而不粗糙，细致而不琐碎，⑤具有神形兼备的艺术效果。

Bīngmǎyǒng jùyǒu shén xíng jiānbèi de yìshù xiàoguǒ.
兵马俑 具有 神 形 兼备 的 艺术 效果。

The horses and warriors of the Terra Otta Army are vivid both in their shapes and expressions.

大　牛：好了，好了，参观兵马俑不简单，还是让我来留个影吧。

韩　佳：好啊。

大　牛：我做准备。准备好了！

韩　佳：准备好了吗，大牛？

大　牛：好了。

韩　佳：我可要照了啊。

Daniel: After I got close to them, I've found these terra cotta warriors are not short at all.

Han Jia: Now you know it. These terra cotta warriors average 1.8 meters in height. The tallest is nearly 2 meters, even taller than you, Daniel.

Daniel: They are really formidable and impressive. You'll never feel tired of looking at them.

Han Jia: Yes. You see the bones of their hand and their fingernails are all delicately made.

Daniel: And the various parts of their bodies are all in proper proportions, making them look like real soldiers.

Han Jia: These terra cotta warriors are very lifelike. Their images may appear simple but not rough, detailed but not redundant. They are vivid both in their shapes and expressions.

Daniel: Yes, indeed. It isn't easy to be able to see such terra cotta warriors, so let me pose for a picture.

Han Jia: Yes.

Daniel: Let me get ready. I'm ready.

Han Jia: Are you ready, Daniel?

Daniel: Yes, please.

Han Jia: I'm going to press the shutter now.

秦始皇兵马俑博物馆外

韩　佳：大牛，感觉怎么样？

大　牛：哎呀呀，真是，哎呀呀！

韩　佳：你怎么又没词了呀？

大　牛：开玩笑。这秦兵马俑不仅仅是罕见的艺术品，它为我们了解
　　　　古代历史提供了非常大的帮助。

韩　佳：没错，通过秦俑坑出土的文物，我们可以了解到当时科技发
　　　　展的水平。

大　牛：简直是举世瑰宝，怎么看也看不够。⑥

韩　佳：那就让我们再次去欣赏一下兵马俑吧。

Han Jia: Daniel, how do you feel?

Daniel: Yeah, yeah, really yeah, yeah.

Han Jia: Short of words again?

Daniel: Kidding. These Qin terra cotta warriors not only are rare works of art, but also have shed new light on the study of ancient history.

Han Jia: Exactly. Through these historical objects unearthed in the pit, we get to know the developments of science and technology in that period.

Daniel: They are world-famous rare treasures, which I never feel tired of seeing.

Han Jia: Now let's recapture the beauty of these terra cotta warriors.

生词 Words and Expressions

1. 奇迹	（名）	qíjì	miracle; wonder; marvel
2. 震惊	（动）	zhènjīng	to shock；to amaze；to astonish
3. 欣赏	（动）	xīnshǎng	to appreciate; to enjoy; to admire
4. 庞大	（形）	pángdà	huge; enormous; colossal; gigantic
5. 威风凛凛		wēi fēng lǐnlǐn	to have an awesome bearing；to have a commanding presence
6. 变化多端		biàn huà duō duān	constantly changing
7. 威武雄壮		wēi wǔ xióng zhuàng	to be full of power and grandeur
8. 百看不厌		bǎi kàn bú yàn	to be worth appreciating a hundred times; can be appreciated a hundred times with delight
9. 罕见	（形）	hǎnjiàn	seldom seen; rare
10. 举世瑰宝		jǔ shì guī bǎo	rarity throughout the world

注释 Notes

1. 你别老"哎呀呀"呀。

   "老"，副词，表示经常、长久。
   The adverb "老" means "always，for long"。
   例如：你不能一天到晚老呆在家里。

2. 你到底想说什么呀？

   "到底"，副词，用在疑问句里，表示进一步追究。
   The adverb "到底" is used in an interrogative sentence to indicate further inquiry.
   例如：你到底去不去？

3. 好庞大的一支军队！

   "好"，副词，表示程度深，多含感叹语气。
   The adverb "好" indicates a high degree and often contains a tone of exclamation.
   例如：好大的雨啊！

4. 就像真的士兵一样。

"像……一样", "像" 是动词, 表示两个事物有较多的共同点, 常和 "一样、这样、那样" 搭配。基本形式是:

像＋名＋一样＋形／动

In the structure "像……一样", the verb "像" indicates that two things share a lot of common ground and often collocates with "一样", "这样" or "那样". The basic pattern is:

像 +noun+ 一样 +adjective/verb

例如: 上海的南京东路像北京的王府井一样繁华。

5. 简洁而不粗糙, 细致而不琐碎。

"而", 连词, 这里连接两个并列的形容词, 表示后一部分补充前一部分。

The conjunction "而" is used here to connect two coordinate adjectives and indicate that the latter complements the former.

例如: 这篇文章短小而生动, 很值得看。

6. 简直是举世瑰宝, 怎么看也看不够。

"简直", 副词, 表示强调夸大的语气, 说明事情或状态达到很高的程度。

The adverb "简直" is used to express an exaggerated tone and indicate that a kind of thing or state has come to a high degree.

例如: 你变化真大, 我简直认不出你来了。

"怎么……也……", 这一结构强调对某种行为或结果的否定, 或者表示不满足, 后面要有否定词 "不／没有"。"怎么……" 表示 "用一切力量"。

The structure "怎么……也……", which must be followed by "不" or "没有", is used to emphasize the negation of some action or result or to express dissatisfaction.

例如: 电脑坏了, 怎么修也修不好。

替换练习　Substitution Drills

1. 兵马俑　　　是　　中国人　　　的骄傲。
　　女儿　　　　　　妈妈
　　他　　　　　　　我们学校
　　长城　　　　　　中华民族

2. 我眼前　　　的这支军队　　锐不可挡。
　　你看到　　　　　　　　　百战百胜
　　他带领　　　　　　　　　战功赫赫
　　走在前面　　　　　　　　威震四海

3. 兵马俑　　　具有　神形兼备　的　艺术效果。
　　这座雕塑　　　　动静结合
　　他的书法　　　　淋漓酣畅
　　这首诗　　　　　情景交融

会话　Conversation

完成下列会话 Complete the following dialogues
（如括号里有词语或提示，请按要求做 Use words or expressions given in the brackets）

A：兵马俑真是了不起！
B：＿＿＿＿＿＿＿＿＿＿＿＿＿＿。（要不然）
A：你们西安人感到很自豪吧？
B：＿＿＿＿＿＿＿＿＿＿＿＿＿＿。

A：专家说兵马俑的艺术价值非常高。
B：＿＿＿＿＿＿＿＿＿＿＿＿＿＿。（怎么……也……）
A：你来西安一趟非常值得吧！再多呆几天嘛。
B：＿＿＿＿＿＿＿＿＿＿＿＿＿＿。（简直）

西安

【第四集】

秦始皇陵下

韩　佳：哎，大牛，来到西安，看过了兵马俑，那你知道它是为谁而
　　　　修建的吗？①

大　牛：为秦始皇②啊，他就是 2200 多年前第一个统一中国的皇帝。

韩　佳：对，那你知道他去世之后葬在什么地方吗？

大　牛：这个嘛，应该在这附近吧？

韩　佳：别找了，我们今天就要去看看秦始皇陵，保证让你大吃一惊。

大　牛：又要让我吃一惊？好，走吧。

Han Jia: Daniel, in Xi'an this time, we've seen the terra cotta warriors. Do you know for whom were they made?

Daniel: For Qin Shihuang. He was the country's first emperor who united China over 2,200 years ago.

Han Jia: Then do you know where he was buried after his death?

Daniel: I guess it should be around here.

Han Jia: Stop looking for it. Today I'll take you to see the Qin Shihuang Mausoleum. And I guarantee you'll be surprised.

Daniel: Me, surprised again? OK, come on.

秦始皇陵的台阶上

大　牛：走了这么长的路，你说的秦始皇陵到底在哪儿啊？

　　　　Nǐ shuō de Qínshǐhuáng Líng dàodǐ zài nǎr a?
　　　　你 说 的 秦始皇 陵 到底 在 哪儿 啊？

Where is the Qin Shihuang Mausoleum you mentioned?

韩　佳：就在我们脚下呀。

大　牛：啊，这座土堆就是陵墓啊？

韩　佳：还不止呢，这里方圆50多公里都是秦始皇陵。

大　牛：怎么可能这么大呢？

韩　佳：怎么不可能？秦始皇陵从秦始皇即位起就开始修建，③前后
　　　　历时38年，比埃及胡夫金字塔修建的时间还要长8年呢。

大　牛：那得用多少人啊？

韩　佳：动用人数最多的时候达到了80万，是埃及胡夫金字塔修建
　　　　人数的8倍。

大　牛：真是一项既罕见又巨大的工程。④

韩　佳：说得没错，不过在这里用"庞大"比较好。⑤"庞大"有太大
　　　　了、大而不当的意思。

大　牛："庞大"，"庞"读二声，"大"读四声，意思是太大了，含有
　　　　贬义。……

韩　佳：那我们到山顶上去看看。

大　牛：走。

Daniel: We've walked a long way, but where on earth is the Qin Shihuang Mausoleum you mentioned?

Han Jia: It's right here underfoot.

Daniel: Is this mound the mausoleum?

Han Jia: Not just that. The whole area within a radius of 50 kilometers lies on top of the mausoleum.

Daniel: It can't be this large!

Han Jia: Why not? The construction of the tomb started as soon as Qin Shihuang took the throne. It took 38 years, eight years more than it took to build Khufu's Pyramid of Egypt.

Daniel: How many people were involved in this project?

Han Jia: At one point, the project used 800,000 workers, eight times as many as the workers used for the construction of Khufu's Pyramid.

Daniel: It was indeed a rare and "juda" project.

Han Jia: You are right. But, here it would be more appropriate to use "pangda" (colossal). "Pangda" means too big or unreasonably large.

Daniel: "Pangda", second tone, fourth tone, means gigantic, colossal. It's a derogatory term. ...

Han Jia: Let's get on the top of the hill to take a look.

Daniel: Let's go.

韩　佳：大牛，咱们身后的是骊山。

大　牛：这儿的景色真不错！秦始皇陵地方选得真好！

韩　佳：哎，皇陵选在这里可不光是因为这里景色好，古代人认为如果把陵墓建在这里，就可以保佑自己的朝代世世代代地传下去。

大　牛：哦，是这样，可是这里好像看不到什么陵园的建筑。

韩　佳：2000多年过去了，秦始皇陵的地面建筑已经不存在了，现代的人根据一些遗迹，勾画出了秦始皇陵当年宏大的规模。

大　牛：那你说说看当年的陵园是个什么样子。⑥

韩　佳：这陵园是仿照秦代都城咸阳建造的，大体上像一个汉字的"回"字，陵墓的周围筑有两重城垣。

大　牛："城垣"就是城墙吗？

韩　佳：对，"垣"就是墙的意思。

大　牛："垣"，读二声，是墙的意思。……虽然这陵园那么大，我看最主要的还是这座像山一样的土堆了。

韩　佳：嗯，没错。秦始皇陵集中了秦代文明的最高成就。

Qínshǐhuáng Líng jízhōngle Qíndài wénmíng de zuì gāo chéngjiù.
秦始皇　陵　集中了　秦代　文明　的　最　高　成就。

The Qin Shihuang Mausoleum embodies the greatest cultural achievements of the Qin Dynasty.

Han Jia: Daniel, behind us is the Lishan Mountain.

Daniel: The scenery is pretty good. It is a nice site chosen for the mausoleum.

Han Jia: The site for the tomb was chosen to be here not just because of the nice scenery here.Ancient people believed the site for the tomb would bless the dynasty, ensuring that it would last generation after generation.

Daniel: Oh, I see. But I could hardly see anything substantial related to the mausoleum.

Han Jia: After more than 2,000 years, the ground structures of the mausoleum have disappeared. Based on the remnants, contemporary artists reproduced

on canvas the grandeur of the mausoleum.

Daniel: Then, please tell us what the mausoleum looked like originally.

Han Jia: The mausoleum was built in imitation of Xianyang, the capital of the Qin Dynasty. It was basically like the Chinese character "hui" (double squares with one inside the other). The tomb was surrounded with two walls.

Daniel: Does "chengyuan" mean a city wall?

Han Jia: Yes, "yuan" means a wall.

Daniel: "Yuan", second tone, means wall. ... Despite its large size, I find the principal part of this mausoleum is this hill-like earthen mound.

Han Jia: Exactly. The Qin Shihuang Mausoleum embodies the greatest cultural achievements of the Qin Dynasty.

韩　佳：秦始皇生前就非常奢华，死后这巨大的风土也显现出了他的尊威。

大　牛：的确！我们身后的这座土堆就像金字塔。

韩　佳：嗯，古埃及的金字塔是世界上最大的地上王陵，而我们中国的秦始皇陵是世界上最大的地下皇陵。这巨大的风土还有一个作用，就是保护下面的地宫。

大　牛：啊，还有地宫呢？我们赶紧去看看吧！

韩　佳：哎，不能看，现在的技术还发掘不了，所以真正的皇陵地宫我们现在是看不到的。

大　牛：啊，现在还看不到？真是太可惜了！

韩　佳：可惜什么呀，让这些文物好好地保存在地下不是很好吗？如果你想知道这皇陵地宫是什么样子，我可以给你讲讲史书上是怎么记载的。

大　牛：好啊。

韩　佳：史书上记载，地宫里有以水银表现的江河大海，⑦宫顶上装饰着天文星宿之象，地面有模拟统一的中国疆土，还有用鲸鱼油做成的长明灯，照亮了整个宫殿，经久不息。

大　牛：嗯，用水银做成的江河，想想都觉得很神秘。

韩　佳：是啊，这秦始皇陵还有很多秘密要等待人们去揭开呢。

Zhèli háiyǒu hěn duō mìmì děngdài rénmen qù jiēkāi ne.
这里 还有 很 多 秘密 等待 人们 去 揭开 呢。

There are still many mysteries waiting to be uncovered here.

Han Jia: Qin Shihuang lived an extravagant life when he was alive. So after his death, this huge mound was built to symbolize his dignity and authority.

Daniel: Yes, indeed. The mound behind us looks like a pyramid.

Han Jia: The pyramids of ancient Egypt are the largest imperial tombs above ground. And China's Qin Shihuang Mausoleum is the largest imperial tomb underground. This huge mound has another function, that is to protect the underground palace.

Daniel: Wow, there is an underground palace? Come on, let's go and take a look.

Han Jia: Oh, no. You can't see it. The current technologies are still incapable of excavating it. So the real underground palace is still not ready for us to see.

Daniel: Oh, we can't see it now. What a pity!

Han Jia: It isn't a pity. Isn't it good to have all the cultural relics safely preserved underground? If you really want to know what the underground palace looks like, I can tell you a bit according to the records in historical books.

Daniel: OK.

Han Jia: According to historical records, there are rivers and oceans in the form of mercury in the palace. The ceiling of the palace is decorated with an astronomical chart. On the floor, there should be a simulated map of a unified China. There is also an altar lamp burning whale oil. The lamp is supposed to burn eternally to keep the entire palace bright.

Daniel: What, rivers of mercury? It sounds so mysterious.

Han Jia: Yes, indeed. There are still a lot of mysteries about the Qin Shihuang Mausoleum waiting to be uncovered.

秦始皇陵的园林内

大　牛：秦始皇陵的神秘之处真是太多了！
韩　佳：给人以想象的空间不是很好吗？
大　牛：真希望秦始皇陵打开以后我也能看到。
韩　佳：没问题，有机会的。

Daniel: There are indeed lots of mysteries about it.

Han Jia: It's not bad to leave room for imagination.

Daniel: I do wish I could see it after the Qin Shihuang Mausoleum is opened.

Han Jia: No problem. It's possible.

生 词 Words and Expressions

1. 修建	（动）	xiūjiàn	to build；to construct；to erect
2. 葬	（动）	zàng	to bury；to inter
3. 大吃一惊		dà chī yì jīng	to be greatly surprised；to be quite taken aback
4. 陵墓	（名）	língmù	mausoleum；tomb
5. 不止	（动）	bùzhǐ	not to stop；not limited to
6. 贬义	（名）	biǎnyì	derogatory sense
7. 仿照	（动）	fǎngzhào	to imitate；to follow
8. 奢华	（形）	shēhuá	luxurious；sumptuous；extravagant
9. 经久不息		jīng jiǔ bù xī	prolonged

注释 Notes

1. 那你知道它是为谁而修建的吗？

"为……而……"："为"，介词，表示后边动作的目的；"而"，连词，把前面表示目的的成分连接到动词上面。

In the structure "为……而……", the preposition "为" indicates the objective of the verb following it，and the conjunction "而" is used to connect the objective with the verb.

例如：为取得更好的学习成绩而努力。

2. 秦始皇

秦始皇（公元前 259 - 公元前 210)，即嬴政。战国时期秦国的国君，后来统一中国，建立了秦王朝，成为中国历史上第一个统一的中央集权的封建国家。

The First Emperor of Qin，namely Ying Zheng (259-210 BC)，was the monarch of Qin during the Warring States Period. Later he unified China and founded the Qin empire，the first united，centralized and feudal state in Chinese history.

3. 秦始皇陵从秦始皇即位起就开始修建。

"从……起……"，表示开始时间或起点的范围。

"从……起……" indicates the starting time or its range.

例如：从明天起学校正式开学。
　　　保护环境要从自己做起。

4. 真是一项既罕见又巨大的工程。

"既……又……"，这一结构表示两种情况都有。

The structure "既……又……" indicates that both situations exist.

例如：这件衣服既漂亮又便宜。

5. 不过在这里用"庞大"比较好。

"不过"，连词，表示转折，这里用来补充、修正上文的意思。比"但是"轻。多用于口语。

The conjunction "不过"，denoting transition，is used here to complement and revise what has been said above. It is gentler than "但是" and is mostly used in oral Chinese.

例如：小王工作很努力，不过性子太急。

6. 那你说说看当年的陵园是个什么样子。

"说说看"，"看"在这里是助词，用在动词重叠式后面表示尝试。

In the structure "说说看"，"看" is a function word and is used after a structure of duplicate verbs to indicate an attempt.

例如：这种水果味道很好，你尝尝看。

7. 地宫里有以水银表现的江河大海。

"以"，介词，为文言词，用于书面语，意思是"拿，用"。

The verb "以"，meaning "拿，用"(with)，is a word in classical Chinese and is used in the written language.

例如：他在学习中以顽强的毅力克服了各种困难。

替换练习 Substitution Drills

1. 你说的　　秦始皇陵　　到底在　　哪儿　　　　啊?
　　　　　　兵马俑　　　　　　　　什么地方
　　　　　　九寨沟　　　　　　　　哪个省
　　　　　　金字塔　　　　　　　　哪个国家

2. 秦始皇陵　集中了　　秦代　　文明　　的最高成就。
　　十三陵　　　　　　明代　　科学
　　颐和园　　　　　　清代　　艺术
　　金字塔　　　　　　古埃及　技术

3. 这里还有很多　秘密　　等待人们去　　揭开　　呢。
　　　　　　　　宝藏　　　　　　　　　挖掘
　　　　　　　　荒地　　　　　　　　　开垦
　　　　　　　　资源　　　　　　　　　利用

会话 Conversation

完成下列会话 Complete the following dialogues
(如括号里有词语或提示,请按要求做 Use words or expressions given in the brackets)

A: 你看这秦始皇陵怎么样?

B: ＿＿＿＿＿＿＿＿＿＿＿＿＿＿＿。(既……又……)

A: 你知道修建秦始皇陵用了多长时间?

B: ＿＿＿＿＿＿＿＿＿＿＿＿＿＿＿。(猜猜看)

A: 秦始皇陵的地下部分为什么还没挖掘呢?

B: ＿＿＿＿＿＿＿＿＿＿＿＿＿＿＿。(由于)

A: 现在能知道地下部分的大概情况吗?

B: ＿＿＿＿＿＿＿＿＿＿＿＿＿＿＿。(根据)

韩　佳：在西安有一座专门陈列文字的博物馆。

大　牛：什么，什么？ 等等！陈列文字的博物馆？ 那不就是图书馆吗？

韩　佳：可以说是图书馆，但又不是。

大　牛：你今天这么神秘，到底是什么博物馆？

韩　佳：西安碑林博物馆。

Han Jia: In Xi'an, there is a museum, in which only written materials are on display.

Daniel: What? Wait a minute. A museum of written materials? Is it a library?

Han Jia: You may say so. But actually it isn't a library.

Daniel: You sound so mysterious today. What kind of museum is it exactly?

Han Jia: Xi'an Forest of Stone Steles Museum.

碑林博物馆第一展室

大　牛：好多石碑呀！

韩　佳：这是唐代撰写的十二部经书①，这些经书是中国古代知识分子必读的。

Zhèxiē jīngshū shì Zhōngguó gǔdài zhīshi fènzǐ bì dú de.
这些　经书　是　中国　古代　知识　分子　必　读　的。

These are the classics, which ancient Chinese intellectuals considered to be compulsory reading material.

韩　佳：在唐朝的时候，印刷术还不是那么发达，人们读书都是靠手抄写，一抄多了难免会出现错误，②为了有一个标准的版本，这部石刻经书就诞生了。

大　牛：哦，原来是这样。③的确，把正确的经文刻在石头上大家都能来看，而且还能永久保存。④

韩　佳：这个办法不错吧。这些石碑上刻有 65 万字，可以称得上是最重最大的图书了，⑤所以别人都管这里叫"石制图书馆"⑥。

Daniel: So many stone steles.

Han Jia: These are the 12 classics all engraved in the Tang Dynasty. These are the classics, which ancient Chinese intellectuals considered to be the compulsory reading materials.

Han Jia: During the Tang Dynasty, printing wasn't quite advanced yet. The books people read were all copied by hand. It was unavoidable to make mistakes. To have a standard version of these classics, classics carved in stone were thus born.

Daniel: Oh, I see. Yes, authentic classics carved in stone could be not only read by all people, but also preserved forever.

Han Jia: This was indeed a novel idea. Bearing a total of 650,000 characters, these steles may be the heaviest and biggest books in the world. So some people also call this museum a stone book library.

大　牛：你看，大秦景教流行中国碑。

韩　佳：这"大秦"是中国古代对东罗马的称呼，"景教"是基督教
　　　　的一个流派，这块石碑上面记载的是唐代时基督教传入中国
　　　　的一些情况！

大　牛：很有意思。你看，上面还有西方文字呢！

韩　佳：据推测，这些是古叙利亚文。怎么样，很感兴趣吧？

大　牛：要是读读它就能了解中国古代文化交流的情况。

韩　佳：啊，你看得懂啊？

大　牛：这个嘛，再研究研究。

韩　佳：嗨，你别研究了，这碑林里还有很多吸引人的地方呢。

Daniel: Look at this stele describing the religion of Daqin *Jingjiao* in China.

Han Jia: In ancient China, Daqin referred to Eastern Rome. *Jingjiao* was a Christian sect. This stele records how Christianity was introduced in China in the Tang Dynasty.

Daniel: Very interesting. Look, there are even Western characters there.

Han Jia: According to inference, they are ancient Syrian. Well, is it interesting?

Daniel: If we could read them, we'd understand ancient China's cultural exchanges with the outside world.

Han Jia: Oh, are you able to read them?

Daniel: I still need further study.

Han Jia: Hey, you'd better stop your study. There are still a lot of more interesting things about these steles here.

禮記卷第七 謂由也而不知禮乎 晏朝而退孔子聞之曰誰 事交乎階質明而始行事 祭子路與室事交乎戶堂 臨祭其為不敬大矣他日 心皆倦怠矣有司跛倚以 燭雖有強力之容肅敬之 速闇而祭日不足繼之 禮子路為季氏宰繼之 具矣不足以饗帝毋輕議 饗之禮不足以饗帝大旅

大　牛：哎哟，好漂亮的字啊！

韩　佳：嗯，漂亮吧！这里有很多中国著名书法家的作品，比如苏东坡、黄庭坚、米芾、蔡京。

大　牛：就是说各种各样的书法应有尽有。

Gè zhǒng gè yàng de shūfǎ yīng yǒu jìn yǒu.
各 种 各 样 的 书法 应 有 尽 有。

Here are all the different styles of calligraphy that you could ever wish for.

韩　佳：大牛，你看。

大　牛：这不就是一幅画吗，画的是竹子？

韩　佳：你再仔细看看。

大　牛：咦，这竹叶合起来是一个一个的字！

韩　佳：嗯。

大　牛：这里写的是什么？

韩　佳：这是一首描写竹子清高品格的诗。

大　牛：把诗藏在画里，这种创意太棒了！我特别喜欢这个作品。

韩　佳：哎，它把文字和绘画结合在一起，所以就叫"藏诗画"。像这样的作品这里还有一些呢，我们慢慢看吧。

Daniel: Wow, how beautiful the calligraphy is!

Han Jia: Beautiful? There're works by many famed Chinese calligraphers, such as Su Dongpo, Huang Tingjian, Mi Fu and Cai Jing.

Daniel: Here are all the different styles of calligraphy that you could ever wish for.

Han Jia: Daniel, look.

Daniel: Isn't this a picture of bamboos?

Han Jia: Look carefully.

Daniel: Oh, these bamboo leaves are actually characters if put together.

Han Jia: Yeah.

Daniel: What's written here?

Han Jia: It's a poem praising the fine qualities of bamboos.

Daniel: Hiding the poem in a picture is really an ingenious idea. I like this work very much.

Han Jia: Yeah. A picture combined with words is called a poem-hiding picture. There are still some more of such works here. Let's just enjoy them slowly.

韩　佳：在宋代⑦有一群文人学者为了挽救文化，将碑石运到了这里，这就是中国历史上第一次大规模收藏碑石的行动，再加上后人悉心地搜集和保护，才有了这里3000多方碑石。

大　牛：韩佳，你说错了吧？应该说"细心"才对。

韩　佳：我说的是"悉心"，是指用尽所有精力的意思，和"细心"是不一样的。

大　牛：哦，原来是两个词。"悉心"，都读一声，是指用尽所有精力的意思。……"细心"，"细"读四声，"心"读一声，是小心谨慎的意思。……

韩　佳：嗯，没错，传统文化需要人们悉心地保护。

Chuántǒng wénhuà xūyào rénmen xīxīn de bǎohù.

传统　文化　需要　人们　悉心　地　保护。

It is necessary for people to devote all their attention to the protection of traditional culture.

韩　佳：大牛，你觉得碑林怎么样啊？

大　牛：本来感觉不错，就是你一直在催我，我还没看够呢！

Han Jia: There was a group of scholars in the Song Dynasty. To resurrect cultural traditions, they brought some past steles here. This was the first large-scale resurrection of steles in Chinese history. Thanks to the "xixin" (first tone) protection and additional collections by people of later generations, it became possible for over 3,000 steles all to be gathered here.

Daniel: Han Jia, you just had a slip of the tongue. You should have said "xixin" (falling tone) instead of "xixin" (first tone).

Han Jia: I said "xixin" (first tone) meaning to devote all of one's energy to something. It's different from the fourth-tone "xixin".

Daniel: Oh, they are actually two different words. "Xixin", two first tones, means to use all one's energy in doing something. ... "Xixin", fourth tone, first tone, is an adverb which means carefully. ...

Han Jia: Yes, exactly. It is necessary for people to devote all their attention to the protection of traditional culture.

Han Jia: Daniel, what do you think of the forest of steles?

Daniel: Actually I like them very much, but you keep pressing me to move on. I really need more time to appreciate them.

生词　Words and Expressions

1. 陈列　（动）　chénliè　to display；to lay out；to exhibit
2. 石碑　（名）　shíbēi　stone tablet；stele
3. 撰写　（动）　zhuànxiě　to write
4. 印刷术　（名）　yìnshuāshù　printing；art of printing
5. 版本　（名）　bǎnběn　edition
6. 流派　（名）　liúpài　school；sect
7. 应有尽有　　yīng yǒu jìn yǒu　to have everything that one could have
8. 清高　（形）　qīnggāo　aloof from petty politics and material pursuits；pure and lofty
9. 挽救　（动）　wǎnjiù　to save；to remedy；to rescue

注释 Notes

1. 经书

　　指《易经》《书经》《诗经》《论语》等中国古代的儒家经传。

　　The Confucian classics include *The Book of Changes*, *The Book of History*, *The Book of Songs*, *The Analects*, etc.

2. 一抄多了难免会出现错误。

　　"一……难免……"，表示一个动作超过了限度就不可避免地产生不好的结果。"一"用来加强语气。

　　The structure "一……难免……" indicates that once an action exceeds the limit，it will cause a bad result．"一" is used to intensify the tone.

　　例如：教育孩子，话一说多了难免引起孩子的反感。

3. 原来是这样。

　　"原来"，副词，表示发现以前不知道的情况，含有恍然醒悟的意思。

　　The adverb "原来" indicates that the formerly-unknown situation has been discovered. It implicates the meaning of waking up to the truth in an instant.

　　例如：我以为他出国留学去了，原来他还在北京。

4．把正确的经文刻在石头上大家都能来看，**而且**还能永久保存。

"而且"，连词，这里连接并列成分，表示意思更进一层。连接小句时，后面常有"还、也、又、更"等。

The conjunction "而且" is used to connect two coordinate components and express a further meaning. When connecting two clauses, it is usually followed by "还""也""又""更" etc.

例如：从这里去西单，坐汽车可以，坐地铁也可以，而且更快。

"而且"的前面常有"不仅、不但"跟它相呼应。参看本书第六集注释3。

"而且" often collocates with preceding words of "不仅" or "不但". (see Note 3 of Section 6)

5．可以**称得上**是最重最大的图书了。

"称得上"，"上"是动词"称"的补语，表示达到一定的标准。"称得上"的意思是"能被称上"，"够资格是……"。

The structure "称得上", in which "上" is the complement of "称", indicates that something has come up to a certain standard. It means "能被称上" or "够资格是……" (to deserve to be called).

例如：他称得上英雄。

否定形式是"称不上"。

The negative form is "称不上".

例如：他称不上模范。

6．别人都**管**这里**叫**石刻图书馆。

"管……叫……"，这个结构用来指称人或事物，用于口语。

The structure "管……叫……", a colloquial expression, is used to indicate a person or thing.

例如：人们管外国货叫洋货。

7．宋代

中国历史上的一个朝代，赵匡胤建立，都城汴梁（今河南开封）。自公元960到1127年称为北宋；1127年到1279年称为南宋，建都临安（今浙江杭州）。

The Song Dynasty, a dynasty in Chinese history, during which the capital of China was Bianliang (today's Kaifeng, Henan Province), was founded by Zhao Kuangyin. From AD 960 to 1127, it was called the Northern Song; from 1127 to 1279, the Southern Song, during which the capital of China was Lin'an (today's Hangzhou, Zhejiang Province).

替换练习 Substitution Drills

1. 这些 ┊ 经书 ┊ 是 ┊ 中国古代知识分子 ┊ 必 ┊ 读 ┊ 的。
   　　　 课程 　　　 外国学生 　　　　　 选
   　　　 知识 　　　 技术工人 　　　　　 备
   　　　 衣物 　　　 游客 　　　　　　　 带

2. 各种各样 ┊ 的 ┊ 书法 ┊ 应有尽有。
   不同风味 　　　 食品
   各种语言 　　　 图书
   各种类型 　　　 玩具

3. 传统文化 ┊ 需要人们 ┊ 悉心 ┊ 地 ┊ 保护。
   外国经验 　　　　　　 认真 　　　 研究
   儒家思想 　　　　　　 批判 　　　 继承
   高端科技 　　　　　　 大胆 　　　 引进

会话 Conversation

完成下列会话 Complete the following dialogues
（如括号里有词语或提示，请按要求做 Use words or expressions given in the brackets）

A: 这石碑上刻的都是中国古代的典籍。
B: ＿＿＿＿＿＿＿＿＿＿＿＿＿＿＿＿。（原来）
A: 你知道孔子吗?
B: ＿＿＿＿＿＿＿＿＿＿＿＿＿＿＿＿。（而且）

A: 听说中国古代的文字都是刻在龟甲和兽骨上的，是吗?
B: ＿＿＿＿＿＿＿＿＿＿＿＿＿＿＿。（管……叫……）
A: 有的还把文字刻在竹片上，那叫什么呢?
B: ＿＿＿＿＿＿＿＿＿＿＿＿＿＿＿。

西安

【第六集】

场景 Scene 陕西历史博物馆外

韩　佳：大牛，你对西安有什么印象啊？

大　牛：都说西安是一座天然的历史博物馆，这句话说得一点儿也不假。这里的历史文物、名胜古迹，真是令人吃惊。

韩　佳：说到这博物馆啊，① 我们今天就要去陕西历史博物馆参观参观。在那里啊，您能看到很多……

大　牛：哎，韩佳别说了，我们还是亲眼去看看吧。

韩　佳：好。

Han Jia: Daniel, what's your impression about Xi'an?

Daniel: It is surely true that the whole city of Xi'an is a history museum. There are so many fascinating historical relics and ancient sites of cultural interest.

Han Jia: Since you talked about the museum, today we are going to visit the Shaanxi History Museum. There, you will be able to see many ...

Daniel: Han Jia, you'd better stop talking and let's go to see with our own eyes.

Han Jia: OK.

大　牛：这么多青铜器啊!②

韩　佳：早在 3600 多年前，中国就已经有青铜器了，在随后的 1000 多年时间里，中国经历了青铜器时期。在这里呢，您能看到中国古代青铜器中的代表。

大　牛：没错，大家看，这里能看到各种各样的鼎。这鼎在中国古代不仅能用来煮东西，而且它还是一种礼器，③ 象征着权力和尊严。

韩　佳：没错，鼎不只是一种炊具，还是一种礼器。④

Dǐng bùzhǐ shì chuījù, hái shì yì zhǒng lǐqì.
鼎 不只 是 炊具，还 是 一 种 礼器。

Ding were used not only in cooking, but also for ceremonial purposes.

韩　佳：2000 多年前正是青铜器的鼎盛时期。

大　牛：我们接着参观吧。

Daniel: There are so many bronze objects here.

Han Jia: As early as 3,600 years ago, bronze objects were already made in China. And in the ensuing 1,000 years, China witnessed a bronze age. Here, you can see various exemplary bronze objects of ancient China.

Daniel: Yes. Please look. Here, we can see a variety of bronze cooking vessels, known as *ding*. The *ding* bronze objects were used in ancient China not only as a cooking utensil but also as a sacrificial vessel symbolizing power and dignity.

Han Jia: Exactly, *ding* was used not only as a cooking utensil, but also for ceremonial purposes. Bronze objects had their heyday over 2,000 year ago.

Daniel: Let's see this side.

场景 Scene 陕西历史博物馆第三展厅

韩　佳：大牛，这一路看了这么多文物，你知道我们都走过了几个时
　　　　期吗？

大　牛：最早的陶器应该是远古时期的吧，然后是 2000 多年前的青
　　　　铜器，秦代、汉代的铁器和建筑都十分突出，然后是那些具
　　　　有不同民族风格的文物，都是民族大融合时期留下来的，再
　　　　接着就是中国古代最鼎盛的朝代——

合：唐代。

Han Jia: Daniel, we've seen so many relics, but do you know how many eras we have visited so far?

Daniel: The earliest was the pottery era in prehistoric times. Then the Bronze Age over 2,000 years ago. And in the Qin and Han Dynasties, their iron tools and architecture were quite outstanding. Then the various historical relics, featuring different ethnic styles. They came from the periods when different ethic groups lived harmoniously. And then it was ancient China's most prosperous period—

Chorus: The Tang Dynasty.

大　牛：方方正正的，像个棋盘。

韩　佳：这就是当时世界上最大的城市之一了，面积是后来明代西安的 8 倍，人口上百万呢。

大　牛：一百万就一百万嘛，还非要说"上百万"？⑤

韩　佳：在汉语里啊，"上"根据搭配词语的不同呢，它的含义也是不同的。在这里，"上"是表示达到某种程度或者是数量，比如说：上规模、上档次、上千人、上年纪等等。

大　牛：哦，明白了。在这里，"上"是表示达到某种程度或数量。例如：唐代的长安拥有上百万的人口。

Tángdài de Cháng'ān yōngyǒu shàng bǎiwàn rénkǒu.
唐代 的 长安 拥有 上 百万 人口。

In the Tang Dynasty Chang'an had a population of one million.

大　牛：这不是唐三彩吗？这个作品看着特别眼熟。

韩　佳：这就是大名鼎鼎的三彩骆驼载乐俑，非常的精彩！你看这骆驼，驼着八个奏乐载舞的人。你仔细看会发现，这些都是外国友人。

大　牛：从他们的穿着打扮就能看出来，他们和我一样都是外国人。

Daniel: It's a square shape like a checkerboard.

Han Jia: It was then one of the largest cities in the world. It was eight times as large as Xi'an in the Ming Dynasty, with a population of as many as one million.

Daniel: It's just one million, but why did you say"shang baiwan"?

Han Jia: In Chinese, the word"shang" may have different meanings, depending on the collates it goes with. Here it means "reaching certain degree or certain amount". For instance, "shang guimo" (reaching a large scale); "shang dangci" (reaching a high degree); "shang qian ren" (up to 1,000 people) and "shang nianji" (reaching an old age).

Daniel: Oh, I see. Here "shang" means "to reach a certain extent or a certain number". For example, in the Tang Dynasty Chang'an had a population of one million or so.

Daniel: Is this a tri-color glazed pottery object of the Tang Dynasty? This work of art looks so familiar.

Han Jia: This is the famous tri-color glazed camel carrying musicians. It's fantastic! This camel carries eight musicians and dancers. If you look carefully, you'll find all of them are foreigners.

Daniel: Judging from their attire, we can see that they are all foreigners like me.

陕西历史博物馆第三展厅

韩　佳：经过了青铜器时代、铁器时代，接下来呢，就是黄金时代了。这里有大量唐代的金银器，从这些上面我们就可以看出，唐代的对外交流十分广泛。

大　牛：韩佳，这只能看出来当时的中国很富有，哪里看得出来交流广泛呢？

韩　佳：这你就有所不知了吧！从这些金银器身上我们就可以看到，它运用了很多西方金银器的制作手法，比如掐丝啊、镶嵌啊，都是从别人那儿学来的。

大　牛：原来是这么回事！看来在唐代，中国就十分注重对外交流和借鉴。

Zhōngguó shífēn zhùzhòng duìwài jiāoliú hé jièjiàn.
中国　十分　注重　对外 交流 和 借鉴。

China attached great importance to foreign exchanges and learning from the experiences of other countries.

Han Jia: After the Bronze Age and the Iron Age came the Gold Era. There are a large number of gold and silver objects of the Tang Dynasty here. Judging from some of the gold and silver works, we can see there were extensive exchanges with the outside world during the Tang Dynasty.

Daniel: Han Jia, we can only see from them that China was quite wealthy then, but why did you say exchanges with the outside world were very extensive then?

Han Jia: You don't know about this. From these gold and silver objects, we can see that many Western methods were used in making these gold and silver objects, such as the filigree and inlay techniques, which were all adopted from abroad.

Daniel: Oh, I see. It seems that during the Tang Dynasty, China attached great importance to foreign exchanges and learning from experience of other countries.

陕西历史博物馆第三展厅

大　牛：没想到从那些小小的文物里，就能看出那么有意思的事情来。

韩　佳：没错，这陕西历史博物馆是一个汇聚历史珍宝的地方。

大　牛：韩佳，谢谢你今天给我讲了那么多。

韩　佳：其实啊，这里还有很多珍贵的文物，那我们就留给观众朋友们自己慢慢欣赏吧。

Daniel: I didn't expect that from these small objects we could learn so many interesting things.

Han Jia: Exactly, the Shaanxi History Museum is a place of historical treasures.

Daniel: Han Jia, thanks a lot for telling me so much.

Han Jia: In fact, there are many other valuable relics here. We'll leave them for our audience to appreciate.

生词 Words and Expressions

1. 青铜器 （名） qīngtóngqì bronze ware
2. 礼器 （名） lǐqì sacrificial vessel
3. 象征 （动、名） xiàngzhēng to symbolize，to stand for；symbol
4. 尊严 （名） zūnyán dignity；honor
5. 鼎盛 （形） dǐngshèng prosperous；flourishing
6. 陶器 （名） táoqì pottery；earthenware
7. 融合 （动） rónghé to mix together；to fuse；to merge
8. 大名鼎鼎 dà míng dǐngdǐng famous；celebrated；well-known
9. 广泛 （形） guǎngfàn broad；extensive；widespread
10. 珍宝 （名） zhēnbǎo precious jewelry；treasure

注释 Notes

1. 说到这博物馆啊……

"到"，常用做动词的补语，表示动作达到了目的或有了结果，或动作涉及某人某事。

"到" is often used as the complement of a verb to indicate that an action has attained its goal or got its result，or it involves somebody or something.

例如：他听到得奖的消息高兴得跳了起来。

2. 这么多青铜器啊！

"这么"，代词，表示对数量、程度等的强调。

The pronoun "这么" is used to intensify the quantity or degree.

例如：这孩子都这么高了，长得真快！

3. 这鼎在中国古代不仅能用来煮东西，而且它还是一种礼器。

连词"不仅"和"而且"呼应，构成的"不仅……而且……"结构与"不但……而且……"的意义和用法相当，用于表示递进关系的复句中。"不仅"首先引出第一层意思，"而且"介绍出在程度上更进一步的第二层意思。

The structure "不仅……而且……"，the meaning and usage of which are equivalent to those of "不但……而且……", is used in a progressive complex sentence. "不仅" introduces the first clause, and "而且" introduces the second one, indicating a further meaning.

例如：这里不仅环境优美，而且交通也很方便。

4．鼎不只是一种炊具，还是一种礼器。

"不只……还……"，这一结构强调有进一层意思。

The structure "不只……还……" emphasizes that the subject before it has a further meaning.

例如：他不只是一位医生，还是一位诗人。

城市不只需要建设，还需要爱护。

5．一百万就一百万嘛，还非要说"上百万"？

"就"，副词，"A 就 A"这种格式表示容许或无所谓。

The structure "A 就 A", in which "就" is an adverb, indicates permission or indifference.

例如：买就买吧，只要你喜欢。

"非要"，表示一定要这样。

"非要" means "simply must".

例如：天这么冷，他非要去游泳。

替换练习 Substitution Drills

1. 鼎 　　不只是　　炊具，　　还是一种　　礼器。
   自行车　　　　　交通工具　　　　　健身用品
   电脑　　　　　　书写工具　　　　　通讯设施
   这种台灯　　　　照明用具　　　　　装饰品

2. 唐代　的　长安　拥有　上百万　人口。
   过去　　　北京　　　上千条　胡同
   明代　　　南京　　　上万家　商店
   今天　　　颐和园　　上万棵　树木

3. 中国十分注重　对外交流　　和　　借鉴。
   　　　　　　　改革　　　　　　开放
   　　　　　　　引进　　　　　　吸收
   　　　　　　　继承　　　　　　发展

会话 Conversation

完成下列会话 Complete the following dialogues
（如括号里有词语或提示，请按要求做 Use words or expressions given in the brackets）

A：你见过中国古代的鼎吗？

B：_____。（说到）

A：鼎有几千年的历史了。

B：_____。（这么）

A：这是鼎的仿制品，你想买吗？

B：_____。

A：价钱很贵啊！

B：_____。（……就……）

西安

【第七集】

【场景 Scene】 大慈恩寺外

大　牛：观众朋友们，你们一定认识我身后的这座建筑吧。

韩　佳：这就是西安的标志——大雁塔，也是我们今天的
　　　　目的地。

大　牛：让我们马上出发。

韩　佳：走。

Daniel: Ladies and gentlemen, you must be familiar with this structure behind me.

Han Jia: This is Xi'an's landmark, Dayan Pagoda. It is also our destination for today.

Daniel: Let's get moving.

Han Jia: Let's go.

大慈恩寺内，背景大雁塔

韩　佳：这大雁塔啊……

大　牛：哎，停！我来说。

韩　佳：好，你说。

大　牛：听着啊，大雁塔是唐代的时候建造的，塔高 64.5 米，一共有 7 层。讲解到此结束，谢谢各位。

韩　佳：啊？这就完了？

大　牛：完了，我就知道那么多，接下来该你了。①

韩　佳：我还以为他知道多少呢！这大雁塔呢又叫"大慈恩寺塔"，是唐代的玄奘大师亲自设计的。在历史上玄奘大师对中国的文化作出了重大的贡献。

Xuánzàng dàshī duì Zhōngguó wénhuà zuòchūle zhòngdà gòngxiàn.
玄奘　大师　对　中国　文化　作出了　重大　贡献。

The Monk Xuanzang made great contributions to Chinese culture.

大　牛：咦，玄奘大师！这个名字听起来耳熟。他是谁来着？②

韩　佳：唐僧，你不是很熟悉吗？

大　牛：知道，就是《西游记》里那个既善良又会念咒语的唐三藏。原来大雁塔是他设计的！

韩　佳：《西游记》里的唐僧和真实的玄奘还是有区别的，玄奘是一个博学多识、意志坚强的人。

大　牛：这个我知道，你看他一路上经历了八十一种磨难，最后还是去西天取回了真经，真是了不起！回来后还修建了一座塔。

韩　佳：大牛，不能把小说当成历史来看！看来啊，我得给你好好讲讲这玄奘和大雁塔的故事了，走吧。

Han Jia: About Dayan Pagoda...

Daniel: Halt, halt. Let me say it.

Han Jia: Yeah, please go ahead.

Daniel: Listen to me. Dayan Pagoda was built in the Tang Dynasty. It is 64.5 meters in height, with seven storeys. Well, so much for my explanation. Thank you.

Han Jia: What? That's all?

Daniel: Yes, that's all I know about it. Now you have to take over.

Han Jia: I thought you knew a lot about it. Dayan Pagoda is also called Daci'en Pagoda. It was designed by Great Master Xuanzang of the Tang Dynasty. The Monk Xuanzang made great contributions to Chinese culture.

Daniel: Oh, Great Master Xuanzang! The name sounds so familiar. Who was he?

Han Jia: Tang Seng (Tang Monk). Is it familiar to you?

Daniel: I know. In the novel *Journey to the West,* he is called Tang Sanzang, the kind-hearted monk, who knows how to murmur incantations. I didn't know he designed the pagoda.

Han Jia: The character Tang Seng in *Journey to the West* is different from the real-life Monk Xuanzang. Xuanzang was a knowledgeable and strong-willed man.

Daniel: I know this. You see, on the journey, he experienced 81 kinds of tribulations before successfully obtaining the real Buddhist sutra from India. He was really great! And he built this pagoda after his return.

Han Jia: Daniel, you mustn't take novels as real history. It seems necessary for me to tell you the story about Xuanzang and the Dayan Pagoda. Let's go.

韩　佳：玄奘大师幼年的时候就聪慧过人，所以在十三岁的时候呢，
　　　　就被破格选中成为了僧人。玄奘在学习的过程中发现，翻译
　　　　成汉文的典籍资料还不够。于是呢，他就决心到遥远的印度
　　　　去学习，③ 一路上经过了十几个国家。他历尽艰难，最后终
　　　　于到达了目的地。

Tā　lìjìn　jiānnán, zuìhòu zhōngyú dàodále　mùdìdì.
他 历尽 艰难， 最后　 终于　 到达了 目的地。

After having experienced all kinds of hardships, he eventually
reached his destination.

大　牛：哎，韩佳，这些雕刻都是玄奘大师去印度取经的过程吧？

韩　佳：没错！玄奘的这次旅途啊有四五万公里长，花了整整19年
　　　　的时间，最后回到了长安。明代的小说家吴承恩就是根据玄
　　　　奘法师的这次经历而创作出了《西游记》。

大　牛：哦，原来中国古代四大名著之一《西游记》是这么来的。那
　　　　玄奘回到长安之后呢？

韩　佳：我带你去看看他回到长安之后的情景吧。

大　牛：好。

Han Jia: Xuanzang was unusually bright when he was still a little child. So when he was 13, he was chosen as a monk as an exception. In his studies, Xuanzang found that Buddhist materials translated into Chinese were often inadequate. So he decided to go to the far-away India to study. On his way, he passed through more than ten countries. After having experienced all kinds of hardships, he eventually reached his destination.

Daniel: Hey, Han Jia, are these sculptures about the experiences Great Master Xuangzang had on his way to India?

Han Jia: Exactly. Xuanzang's journey covered a total distance of about 50,000 kilometers. The whole trip took him 19 years before he returned to Chang'an. Wu Cheng'en, a Ming Dynasty novelist, wrote the novel *Journey to the West* based on Monk Xuanzang's experiences on his jurney.

Daniel: Oh, that's how *Journey to the West,* one of the four greatest ancient Chinese novels, was written. Then what happened after Xuanzang's return to Chang'an?

Han Jia: Let me take you to see what happened after his return to Chang'an.

Daniel: Okay.

般若殿内壁画前

大　牛：有这么多人来迎接玄奘大师啊！

韩　佳：嗯，玄奘的这次旅行啊轰动了整个唐王朝。他带回来了600多部经书、文献和许多珍贵的物品。

大　牛：可东西那么多，哪放得下啊？

韩　佳：这就和大雁塔有关了呀。

大　牛：我知道了，玄奘修建大雁塔是为了存放经书。

韩　佳：对，玄奘回国之后，皇帝修建了慈恩寺，玄奘就是第一任住持。他亲自设计并建造了大雁塔，用来保存和翻译经书、文献。

大　牛：原来大雁塔是这么来的。

韩　佳：对，玄奘是中国历史上伟大的翻译家，他制定的翻译规则到今天还在使用，所以玄奘在人们心目中地位崇高。

Xuánzàng zài rénmen xīnmù zhōng dìwèi chónggāo.
玄奘　在　人们　心目　中　地位　崇高。

The image of Xuanzang enjoys a high status in the hearts of the people.

韩　佳：这下你了解了玄奘大师的故事和大雁塔的来历了吧？④

大　牛：这下我了解了。

Daniel: So many people were meeting this monk!

Han Jia: Yeah. Xuanzang's journey caused quite a stir in the Tang Empire. He brought back over 600 scriptural books and documents and many valuable articles.

Daniel: With so many things, where should he put them?

Han Jia: That's why Dayan Pagoda was built.

Daniel: Oh, I know. Xuanzang built the pagoda in order to have a place for his Buddhist books.

Han Jia: Yes. After Xuanzang's return from abroad, the emperor built Ci'en Temple and appointed Xuanzang its first abbot. He designed and built Dayan Pagoda so that he could have a place to keep these books and translate them into Chinese.

Daniel: Oh, that's how the pagoda came into existence.

Han Jia: Yeah, Xuanzang was a great translator in Chinese history. The rules he set up for translation are still in use today. So the image of Xuanzang enjoys a high status in the hearts of the people. Now you understand story about Master Monk Xuanzang and why Dayan Pagoda was built?

Daniel: Yes, I do understand now.

大雁塔下

大　牛：了解了这么多，再看这大雁塔，感觉又不一样。

韩　佳：是吗？怎么不一样啊？

大　牛：怎么说呢，好像更高了。

韩　佳：是啊，这西安大雁塔啊，不仅记录了玄奘大师的功绩，同时呢，也见证了西安1400多年来的历史。⑤

Daniel: With so much background information, now I feel quite different when I see Dayan Pagoda again.

Han Jia: Really? How different?

Daniel: How should I put it? It seems even higher.

Han Jia: Yeah. Xi'an's Dayan Pagoda not only records the deeds of Master Monk Xuanzang, but also has witnessed Xi'an's 1,400 odd years of history.

生词 Words and Expressions

1. 标志　（名、动）　biāozhì　　sign，mark，symbol；to indicate，to mark，to symbolize
2. 咒语　（名）　zhòuyǔ　　incantation；charm
3. 博学多识　bó xué duō shí　learned and versatile
4. 破格　（动）　pògé　　to break a rule；to make an exception
5. 典籍　（名）　diǎnjí　　ancient codes and records；ancient books and records
6. 雕刻　（动）　diāokè　　to carve；to engrave
7. 轰动　（动）　hōngdòng　to cause a sensation；to make a stir
8. 文献　（名）　wénxiàn　document；literature
9. 珍贵　（形）　zhēnguì　valuable；precious
10. 崇高　（形）　chónggāo　lofty；sublime；high

注释　Notes

1. **接下来该你了。**

　　"该"，动词，这里是"轮到"的意思。
　　The verb "该" here means "轮到" (one's turn comes).
　　例如：一会儿该你发表意见了。

2. **他是谁来着？**

　　"来着"，助词，表示曾经发生过什么事情，用于口语。这句话说的是刚才提到的那个人。
　　The function word "来着"，a colloquial expression，indicates that something has happened. In this sentence，it refers to the person mentioned above.
　　例如：你们最近都忙什么来着？

3. **于是呢，他就决心到遥远的印度去学习。**

　　"于是"，连词，表示后一件事是承接前一件事或是前一件事的结果。
　　The conjunction "于是" indicates that the latter thing continues from the former or is the

result of the former.

例如：听了大家的介绍，于是我又决定跟大家一起去。

4. 这下你了解了玄奘大师的故事和大雁塔的来历了吧？

"下"，量词，"回""次"的意思，用于口语。"这下"即这次，表示即将发生的事。

The measure word "下", a colloquial expression, means "回" or "次". "这下", meaning "this time", introduces something to happen.

例如：这下我们可要好好儿看看雪雕了。

5. 这西安大雁塔啊，不仅记录了玄奘大师的功绩，同时呢，也见证了西安1400多年来的历史。

"不仅"，连词，用法同"不但"，后面和"而且、并且、也、还、又"呼应，用于表示递进关系的复句中。"不仅"首先引出第一层意思，后一小句介绍出在程度上更进一步的第二层意思。

Collocating with "而且", "并且", "也", "还" or "又", the conjunction "不仅", is used in a progressive complex sentence. Its usage is equivalent to that of "不但". "不仅" introduces the first clause, and "而且" introduces the second one, indicating a further meaning.

例如：这里不仅人口众多，物产也很丰富。

替换练习 Substitution Drills

1. 玄奘大师	对	中国文化	作出了	重大	贡献。
秦始皇		中国统一		决定性	
他		学校发展		重要	
这些前辈		改革开放		独特的	

2. 他	历尽艰难，	最后终于	到达	了	目的地。
	经过努力		获得		学位
	克服困难		完成		任务
	积极锻炼		康复		身体

3. 玄奘　　　　在人们心目中　　　地位崇高。
   英雄　　　　　　　　　　　　永远活着
   暴徒　　　　　　　　　　　　如同禽兽
   叛徒　　　　　　　　　　　　一钱不值

会话 Conversation

完成下列会话 Complete the following dialogues
(如括号里有词语或提示，请按要求做 Use words or expressions given in the brackets)

A：《西游记》中的唐僧和玄奘是两回事。
B：＿＿＿＿＿＿＿＿＿＿＿＿＿＿＿＿。（来着）
A：我说《西游记》中的唐僧，你看过这部小说吗？
B：＿＿＿＿＿＿＿＿＿＿＿＿＿＿＿＿。

· ·

A：你去过西安吗？
B：＿＿＿＿＿＿＿＿＿＿＿＿＿＿＿＿。（不仅……而且……）
A：那大雁塔你也看过了？
B：＿＿＿＿＿＿＿＿＿＿＿＿＿＿＿＿。

西安

【第八集】

韩　佳：西安是中华民族重要的发源地，它就好比是一棵大树的树
　　　　根，① 在这里呢，您处处都能发现华夏文明的痕迹。

大　牛：韩佳，这话说得太绝对了吧！你就拿这里来说，只有高山和
　　　　森林，哪有什么文明的痕迹啊？②

韩　佳：你啊，是不见不知道，我这就带你去找找。

大　牛：这里会有什么呢？

Han Jia: Xi'an is an important birthplace of the Chinese nation, just like the main roots of a huge tree. Here you can find everywhere traces of Chinese civilization.

Daniel: Han Jia, you'd better not use absolute terms. For instance, on the mountain and in the forest here, are there any traces of civilization?

Han Jia: Sure. Seeing is believing. Let me take you to see if we can find some.

Daniel: What could we find here?

老子祠门口

大　牛：终于爬上来了。

韩　佳：大牛，这里就是我们的目的地了。

大　牛：啊，这不就是一座道观嘛，这就是你要带我来看的文明的痕迹啊？

韩　佳：对啊，2400多年前，这里就是老子讲学的地方。

大　牛：老子？老子在国外也非常有名！他写的《道德经》被译成许多种不同的文字，他是道家思想的创始人。

Lǎozǐ shì Dàojiā sīxiǎng de chuàngshǐrén.

老子 是 道家 思想 的 创始人。

Lao Zi was the founder of Taoism.

大　牛：他说的话都非常有哲理，有什么"知足""寡欲"，还有"物极必反"什么的。③

韩　佳：你还知道"物极必反"啊？"物极必反"啊就是说事物发展到了极端，就会向相反的方向转化，这在汉语中经常会用到。

大　牛："物极必反"就是说事物发展到了极端，就会向相反的方向转化。……

韩　佳：老子啊，是中国历史上一位伟大的哲学家，他的哲学思想在中国有很大的影响。

大　牛：看来西安真的是处处都有文明的痕迹。

韩　佳：我没说错吧，走。

Daniel: Oh, we've finally climbed up here.

Han Jia: Daniel, this is our destination.

Daniel: Oh, isn't this a Taoist temple? This is the place where you want to show me the traces of civilization?

Han Jia: Yeah. Over 2,400 years ago, Lao Zi taught here.

Daniel: Lao Zi? Lao Zi is also very famous abroad. The book, Tao Te Ching, has been translated into many languages. He was the founder of Taoism. His statements are full of philosophy, such as "content with one's lot", "restraint of desires" and "wu ji bi fan" (a thing will turn into its opposite if pushed too far).

Han Jia: You even know "wu ji bi fan", eh? "Wu ji bi fan" means that when things have reached their extreme, they will turn into their opposites. The phrase is often used in Chinese.

Daniel: "Wu ji bi fan" is a Chinese idiom which means when an action has reached its extreme, there will be an equal and opposite counter reaction. ...

Han Jia: Lao Zi was a great philosopher in Chinese history. His philosophical thinking has exerted a great influence on Chinese society.

Daniel: This does prove that in Xi'an, there are traces of civilization everywhere.

Han Jia: So I didn't say anything wrong. Let's go.

韩　佳：快来看。

大　牛：奇怪，这张石桌怎么被围起来了呀？

韩　佳：这可不是石桌，这是老子磨药的石磨。你敲敲看。

大　牛：怎么像铁锅啊？

韩　佳：敲击它就会发出清脆悦耳的声音来，所以人们就管它叫响石。

大　牛：它为什么会发出这种声音呢？

韩　佳：其实它不是一块普通的石头，而是一块陨石，金属含量非常高，④ 所以敲击它就会发出跟一般石头不一样的声音来。

大　牛：看来这里的东西都很特别。

韩　佳：还有更特别的呢！我带你去看几种珍贵的国宝，走。

Kàn lái zhèli de dōngxi dōu hěn tèbié.
看 来 这里 的 东西 都 很 特别。

All things here seem to be very special.

Han Jia: Look.

Daniel: It's strange. Why is this stone table sealed off?

Han Jia: No, this is not a stone table. It was a millstone used by Lao Zi when grinding medicinal herbs. Just knock at it.

Daniel: Does it sound like an iron pot?

Han Jia: Striking at it produces clear and melodious sounds. So people call it the Sounding Stone.

Daniel: Why does it produce this kind of sounds?

Han Jia: This is no ordinary stone. It's a meteorite, containing lots of metal components. So it can produce sounds different from those of ordinary stones when being struck at.

Daniel: All things here seem to be very special.

Han Jia: There are things you may find more special. Let me take you to see some national treasures. Let's go.

野生动物园饲养保护中心园内

大　牛：韩佳，你不是说要带我看国宝嘛？怎么把我带到动物园里
　　　　来了呀？⑤

韩　佳：这里可不是动物园啊，这里是野生动物饲养保护中心。你看，
　　　　国宝就在那儿。

大　牛：啊，就是那些长嘴大鸟？

韩　佳：那是朱鹮，现在全世界也才只有几百只。

大　牛：怎么会这么稀少呢？

韩　佳：环境恶化造成的呗。在上世纪（20世纪）70年代啊，在野
　　　　外几乎看不到它们的踪影，也就在这里还有一个朱鹮种群。

Daniel: Han Jia, you said you would take me to see some national treasures, but why are you taking me to a zoo here?

Han Jia: This is not a zoo. It is a wildlife breeding and protection center. Look, the national treasures are right over there.

Daniel: You mean those long-beaked birds?

Han Jia: They are crested ibises. There are only a few hundred of them in the world.

Daniel: Why so few?

Han Jia: The cause is the deteriorating environment. In the 1970s, the birds were rarely seen in the wild except here. Thus a habitat of the crested ibises has been preserved.

野生动物园饲养保护中心园内

韩　佳：大牛，快来看羚牛。

大　牛：啊？看起来很温顺嘛。

韩　佳：它看起来虽然温顺，其实啊，脾气大着呢！

大　牛：都说人不可貌相，没想到牛也不可貌相。

韩　佳：就是嘛，不过这种动物啊数量也不多了，又是一种珍稀动物。

大　牛：这儿到底有多少种珍稀动物呢？

Zhèr　dàodǐ　yǒu　duōshao　zhǒng　zhēnxī　dòngwù　ne?
这儿 到底 有　多少　种　珍稀　动物　呢？

How many kinds of rare animals are there here?

韩　佳：5种，还有金丝猴、褐马鸡，和一种人们非常熟悉、非常喜爱的动物。

大　牛：哦，我知道了，大熊猫。

野生动物园饲养保护中心园内

韩　佳：大熊猫啊是最惹人喜爱的动物了！中国秦岭山脉是它们的家。

大　牛：大熊猫憨态可掬的样子真是十分可爱。

韩　佳：早在几十万年前啊，大熊猫就已经存在了，所以呢，人们称它们为"活化石"。它们可是中国特有的野生动物啊！

大　牛：今天看了那么多珍稀动物我真是心满意足。

韩　佳：你是心满意足了，我还意犹未尽呢！

Han Jia: Daniel, come here and see the takins.

Daniel: Wow, they look so tame.

Han Jia: They are seemingly tame, but they have very short tempers.

Daniel: It's said that men can not be judged by their looks, and the same rule also applies to animals.

Han Jia: Right. The number of the world's takins is very limited. So they are also a kind of rare animals.

Daniel: How many kinds of rare animals are there in this place?

Han Jia: Five, including golden monkeys, brown-eared pheasants and another species, which most people are familiar with and love very much.

Daniel: Oh, I know, giant pandas.

Han Jia: Giant pandas are the loveliest animals. They live in the Qinling Mountains of China.

Daniel: They are lovely because of their naive and cute behaviors.

Han Jia: Giant pandas had existed hundreds of thousands of years before. So people call them living fossils. They are a kind of special wild animals peculiar to China.

Daniel: I am satisfied as I have seen so many rare animals today.

Han Jia: You are satisfied, but I feel I'd like to see more.

生词 Words and Expressions

1. 发源　　　（动）　fāyuán　　　　　to rise；to originate
2. 痕迹　　　（名）　hénjì　　　　　　mark；trace；vestige
3. 道观　　　（名）　dàoguàn　　　　　Taoist temple
4. 哲理　　　（名）　zhélǐ　　　　　　philosophic theory；philosophy
5. 清脆悦耳　　　　　qīngcuì yuè'ěr　　clear and melodious
6. 陨石　　　（名）　yǔnshí　　　　　　aerolite；stony meteorite
7. 惹　　　　（动）　rě　　　　　　　　to attract；to cause
8. 憨态可掬　　　　　hān tài kě jū　　　charmingly naive
9. 心满意足　　　　　xīn mǎn yì zú　　　to be perfectly content
10. 意犹未尽　　　　　yì yóu wèi jìn　　　meaning has not been fully expressed

注释 Notes

1. 它就**好比**是一棵大树的树根。

"好比"，动词，表示跟以下所说的一样。

The verb "好比" means "can be compared to or to be just like".

例如：学习好比是攀登高峰，没有坚强的毅力是不行的。

2. 你就**拿**这里**来说**，只有高山和森林，哪有什么文明的痕迹啊？

"拿……来说"，这一结构表示从某个方面提出话题。

The structure "拿……来说" is used to introduce a topic from some aspect.

例如：拿小王来说吧，他每天都要朗读一个小时的英语，所以他的英语非常好。

3. 还有"物极必反"**什么的**。

"什么的"，用于口语，在一个成分或几个并列成分之后，相当于"等等"。

The colloquial expression "什么的", equivalent to "等等", is used after one component or a few coordinate ones.

例如：桌上摆的都是书、报、笔什么的。

4. 其实它不是一块普通的石头，而是一块陨石，金属含量非常高。

"不是……而是……"这一结构表示否定前者肯定后者。

The structure "不是……而是" is used to negate the former and affirm the latter.

例如：他要去的地方不是云南而是贵州。

5. 怎么把我带到动物园里来了呀？

"怎么"，指示代词，表示询问原因，同"为什么"。

The demonstrative pronoun "怎么", equivalent to "为什么", is used to inquire the reason.

例如：他今天怎么没来上课？

替换练习 Substitution Drills

1. 老子	是	道家	思想的创始人。
孔子		儒家	
墨子		墨家	
韩非子等		法家	

2. 看来	这里	的	东西	都很	特别。
	那里		水果		便宜
	山区		居民		贫穷
	农村		孩子		艰苦

3. 这儿	到底有多少	种	珍稀动物	呢？
北京		个	连锁商店	
上海		家	五星级饭店	
学校		台	电脑	

会话 Conversation

完成下列会话 Complete the following dialogues

（如括号里有词语或提示，请按要求做 Use words or expressions given in the brackets）

A：现在来中国旅游的外国人特别多。

B：_____。（拿……来说）

A：哎呀，那么多的人啊！都是哪些国家的人?

B：_____。（来自）

· ·

A：你要买点纪念品带回去吗?

B：_____。（什么的）

A：那是什么? 是真的古代钱币吗?

B：_____。（不是……而是……）

西安

【第九集】

韩　佳：大牛，来到西安，你有没有感受到这里到处都充满了唐代的
　　　　气息啊？

大　牛：当然感受到了！毕竟这里原来是唐朝的首都嘛，^①而唐代又
　　　　是一个那么强盛的朝代。真想知道走在一片唐代园林建筑当
　　　　中，那会是一种什么样的感觉？

韩　佳：我们今天要去的这个地方就能让你想象成为现实。

大　牛：真的吗？那还等什么，赶紧带我去看看！

韩　佳：好，我们这就进入西安大唐芙蓉园。

大　牛：走！

Han Jia: Daniel, here in Xi'an, do you have the feeling that the whole city is tinged with the flavor of the Tang Dynasty?

Daniel: Yes, I do. After all, it was the capital of China in the Tang Dynasty, which was the most prosperous of all Chinese dynasties. I was wondering what it would feel like to be in a Tang-style environment.

Han Jia: The place we are going to visit today will make your dream come true.

Daniel: Really? I can't wait. Hurry and take me there.

Han Jia: Okay, we are about to enter Xi'an's Datang Furong Park.

Daniel: Come on.

园内紫云楼前

大　牛：这座园林可真够华丽啊！②

韩　佳：这是一座以唐代文化为主题的公园，③ 在这里呢，您可以尽
　　　　情地领略唐代的风采。

大　牛：没错，在这里能看到各种各样唐代风格的建筑。

韩　佳：是啊。唐代的建筑啊，规模宏大、色调明快、简洁质朴、
　　　　庄重大方，而且唐代建筑规划得既整齐又严谨。

Tángdài jiànzhù guīhuà de jì zhěngqí yòu yánjǐn.
唐代　建筑　规划　得既　整齐　又严谨。

Tang Dynasty architecture is characterized by its neatness and strictness in layouts and style.

韩　佳：唐代之前啊，中国的建筑主要以突出材料本身的颜色为主，
　　　　到了唐代呢，建筑就多采用红色和白色，这样啊，既整齐又
　　　　悦目，而且还可以表明等级和地位。黄颜色就代表皇室，只
　　　　有皇宫和寺庙才能使用；一般的王府和官员就采用红色、青
　　　　色还有蓝色。这样一眼看去，就能辨别出主人的地位了。④

大　牛：原来还有这样的讲究，挺有趣的。

韩　佳：有趣的还多着呢，我们接着往下看。

Daniel: This is a gorgeous park!

Han Jia: Yeah, it is a theme park of the Tang Dynasty culture. In this park of the Tang Dynasty culture, you can appreciate the architecture of the Tang Dynasty to your heart's content.

Daniel: Absolutely. Here you can see all kinds of architectural styles of the Tang Dynasty.

Han Jia: Yeah. The Tang Dynasty structures are known for their magnificent scales, bright colors and pristine and sublime styles. And the Tang Dynasty architecture is characterized by its neatness and strictness in layouts and style. Before the Tang Dynasty, Chinese architecture gave prominence mainly to the original colors of materials. But in the Tang Dynasty, the main colors in use were red and white to achieve the effects of neatness and esthetic beauty. Besides, colors shouldn't be used indiscriminately. The yellow color, reserved for the imperial family, was used only for imperial palaces and temples. For residences of princes and court officials, red, cyan and blue were used. Thus from the color of the house, one could easilly tell the status of its owner.

Daniel: Oh, there were so many rules about colors. It's really interesting.

Han Jia: There are still more interesting things ahead. Let's go on watching.

场景 Scene 园内荷池桥上

大　牛：韩佳，我去过中国许多园林，我觉得这里和其他地方不一样。

韩　佳：那你说说有什么不一样的。

大　牛：好多园林都是小巧幽深，这座园林不但设计精美，而且布局开阔。

Zhè zuò yuánlín búdàn shèjì jīngměi, érqiě bùjú kāikuò.
这 座 园林 不但 设计 精美，而且 布局 开阔。

Not only is this garden exquisitely designed, it's also very spacious.

韩　佳：这就是唐代的气魄！

大　牛：此情此景只有作一首诗我才能表达出我的心情。

韩　佳：啊？你又要作诗啊？

大　牛：听着！绕池闲步看鱼游。

韩　佳：嗯，听起来还不错！

大　牛：点水蜻蜓款款飞。桃花潭水深千尺，遍插茱萸少一人。

韩　佳：你是把白居易、杜甫、李白、王维的诗各抄了一句，然后呢把它们拼凑在了一起。你以为我听不出来啊？

大　牛：怎么给她听出来了？

韩　佳：不过呢，难得你把这些唐诗都记得那么熟，放过你吧。

Daniel: Han Jia, I have visited many Chinese gardens and parks, but I find this one different from any of others.

Han Jia: Then tell me how different it is.

Daniel: Many of them are small and intricate. Not only is this garden exquisitely designed but also very spacious.

Han Jia: That's the style of the Tang Dynasty architecture.

Daniel: It deserves a poem from me to express my feelings.

Han Jia: What? A poem again?

Daniel: Listen. Walking around the pool to watch the fish...

Han Jia: Sounds good!

Daniel: Hovering dragonflies are skimming the water for fun... The Peach Blossom Pool is a thousand feet deep... Planting herbs everywhere, they find my absence.

Han Jia: You were using a line from each of the poems written by Bai Juyi, Du Fu, Li Bai and Wang Wei to piece them together to form a poem of your own. You thought I couldn't tell it?

Daniel: How did she tell the secret?

Han Jia: But after all, it isn't easy for you to remember these Tang poems so well. I let you off.

场景 Scene	**园内诗峡中**

大　牛：这里到处都是唐诗啊！

韩　佳：这里就是唐诗峡。刚才我们看到的都是唐代的大诗人，你背的那些诗句都是他们的诗句。

大　牛：说起这唐诗啊我可是喜欢得不得了！⑤我背一首给你听一听。

韩　佳：好啊。

大　牛：松下问童子，言师采药去。只在此山中，云深不知处。

韩　佳：哟，没想到大牛还能背唐诗呢。

大　牛：那当然了！甭管理解不理解，我都能背下来。⑥

韩　佳：什么叫"理解不理解都能背下来"啊？那不成死记硬背了吗。

大　牛：死记硬背就死记硬背吧，反正我是背得滚瓜烂熟。⑦

韩　佳：哎，"滚瓜烂熟"啊是形容读书或背书十分流利、熟练，是常用的口头语。

大　牛："滚瓜烂熟"形容读书或背书十分流利。例如：我把唐诗背得滚瓜烂熟。

Wǒ bǎ Tángshī bèi de gǔnguā lànshú.

我　把　唐诗　背　得　滚瓜　烂熟。

I can recite many Tang poems by heart.

Daniel: There are Tang poems everywhere.

Han Jia: Yeah, because this is the Tang Poetry Gallery. The poems we saw just now were all written by great poets of the Tang Dynasty. The lines you recited were all from their poems.

Daniel: Speaking of Tang poems, I must say I like them very much. Now, let me recite one for you.

Han Jia: Go ahead.

Daniel: To my question, the boy under a pine tree said, "My teacher is collecting herbs deep in the mountains somewhere in the clouds."

Han Jia: Hey, I didn't expect Daniel could recite Tang poems.

Daniel: That's for sure. No matter whether I understand or not, I can recite them.

Han Jia: What do you mean by "understand or not"? Is that rote learning?

Daniel: Rote learning isn't bad at all. Anyway, I can recite them "gungua lanshu" (to recite fluently).

Han Jia: Yeah, "gungua lanshu" means "to read or recite some text very fluently". It's a frequently used colloquialism.

Daniel: "Gungua lanshu" describes being able to read or recite very fluently. For example, I can recite many Tang poems very fluently.

【中国旅游 场景 Scene】 园内集市

大　牛：观众朋友们，这大唐芙蓉园里还有一个唐代集市，集市里除
　　　　了有许多手工艺品之外，还有许多我大牛没尝过的小吃。⑧
　　　　集市特别热闹，我们现在就去逛逛吧！

韩　佳：观众朋友们也跟我们一起去逛逛吧。

Daniel: Dear audience, in the Datang Furongyuan Park, there is also a Tang-style market. In addition to a variety of handicrafts, the market also sells snacks Daniel has never tasted before. The market is extremely busy. Let's take a stroll through the market.

Han Jia: Dear audience, come with us for the stroll.

生词 Words and Expressions

1. 感受 （名、动） gǎnshòu experience；to experience，to feel
2. 气息 （名） qìxī flavor；smell
3. 强盛 （形） qiángshèng powerful and prosperous
4. 园林 （名） yuánlín gardens；park
5. 尽情 （副） jìnqíng to one's heart's content；as much as one likes
6. 风格 （名） fēnggé style；manner；mode
7. 突出 （动、形） tūchū to protrude；outstanding
8. 寺庙 （名） sìmiào temple
9. 拼凑 （动） pīncòu to piece together；to knock together；to rig up
10. 死记硬背 sǐ jì yìng bèi to memorize mechanically；to learn by rote；to memorize without understanding

注释 Notes

1. **毕竟**这里原来是唐朝的首都嘛。

"毕竟"，副词，用于陈述句中，表示不管怎么样，事情终归还是这样。

The adverb "毕竟"，meaning "after all, at all，or all in all"，is used in a declarative sentence.

例如：他毕竟是个孩子，有些事情还不懂。

2. 这座园林可真**够**华丽啊！

"够"，副词，表示程度很高。

The adverb "够" indicates that the degree is very high.

例如：这件衣服够漂亮的。

3. 这是一座**以**唐代文化**为**主题的公园。

"以……为……"，这一结构相当于"把……作为……""认为……是……"。

The structure "以……为……" is equivalent to "把……作为……"or"认为……是……"。

例如：这个地区以农业为主。

4. 这样一眼看去，就能辨别出主人的地位了。

"一眼看去"，即看了一眼，表示动作快，时间短。用在句首，后面用看见、看出来。

"一眼看去"，meaning "at a glance"，indicates that the action happens fast and lasts a short time. It is placed at the beginning of a sentence，with "看见" or "看出来" used in the latter half of the sentence.

例如：一眼看去，就看出来跑在前面的是小张。

5．说起这唐诗啊我可是喜欢得不得了！

"起"是"说"的补语，表示动作涉及到某事物。用"起"的动词限于"说、谈、提、问"等少数及物动词。

As the complement of "说"，"起" indicates that an action involves something. The verbs collocating with "起" are confined to a few transitive ones such as "说"，"谈"，"提" and "问"．

例如：小王来信还问起你呢。

提起他我就想起很多过去的事。

"不得了"，这里用做补语，表示程度很深。

"不得了"，used as a complement here，indicates that the degree is very high.

例如：儿子考上了大学，妈妈高兴得不得了。

6．甭管理解不理解，我都能背下来。

"甭"，"不用"的合音词。用于口语，这里表示不需要。

The colloquial expression "甭"，being the syneresis of "不用"，means that it is unnecessary.

例如：这件事我已经知道了，你甭说了。

7．反正我是背得滚瓜烂熟。

"反正"，副词，强调在任何情况下，结论或结果都不会改变。

The adverb "反正" emphasizes that no matter what happens，the conclusion or result will not change.

例如：要去你自己去，反正我不去。

8．集市里除了有许多手工艺品之外，还有许多我大牛没尝过的小吃。

"除了……之外,还……"，这一结构表示在什么之外还有别的，二者是相加关系。

The structure "除了……之外，还……" indicates that in addition to something，there exists something else．They are additive relations.

例如：我们学校除了中国学生以外，还有许多外国学生。

替换练习 Substitution Drills

1. 唐代建筑	规划	得既	整齐	又	严谨。
三峡水坝	修建		壮观		实用
这部电影	拍摄		优美		感人
这项计划	制定		实际		前瞻

2. 这座园林	不但	设计精美，而且	布局开阔。
这座城市		清洁整齐	交通方便
这家医院		设施齐全	服务周到
这些学生		成绩优秀	身体健康

3. 我	把	唐诗	背	得	滚瓜烂熟。
他		地板	擦		干干净净
大牛		钱	花		一分不剩
小王		房间	搞		乱七八糟

会话 Conversation

完成下列会话 Complete the following dialogues
（如括号里有词语或提示，请按要求做 Use words or expressions given in the brackets）

A：我来介绍西安的历史，是很难让你满意的。
B：_____。（毕竟）
A：我虽然是西安人，但不是学历史的。
B：_____。（够）

A：西安还有什么有特色的食品吗？
B：_____。（除了……之外，还……）
A：西安居民早餐都吃些什么？
B：_____。（以……为主）

西安 【第十集】

皮影戏表演

韩 佳：哎，大牛，你今天打扮得可够有民族风味儿的啊！

大 牛：那是，我这一身可是正宗的关中①皮影！我还会唱宛宛腔呢。

韩 佳：哎呀，太棒了！大牛，你快教教我。

观众席

韩 佳：大牛，又做梦呢吧？看把你美的。②你看得那么投入，是不是喜欢上皮影戏了呀？③

大 牛：是啊，是啊。你看这皮影戏，既生动又有趣，再加上宛宛腔就更有韵味了。

韩 佳：看来这大牛对皮影戏还真挺感兴趣的。

大 牛：那当然！我对民间艺术非常感兴趣。

Wǒ duì mínjiān yìshù fēicháng gǎn xìngqù.
我 对 民间 艺术 非常 感 兴趣。
I'm very interested in folk arts.

韩 佳：西安的民间艺术可以说是丰富多彩。

大 牛：都有一些什么呢？

韩 佳：你看，有剪纸啊、秦腔④啊、皮影戏啊。

Han Jia: Hey, Daniel, today you are dressed with a strong national flavor.

Daniel: Sure. I am dressed like a typical character in the Guanzhong area's shadow play. Besides, I can also sing the local *Wanwan* Tune.

Han Jia: Wow, that's fantastic! Daniel, teach me how to sing it, please.

Han Jia: Daniel, you are daydreaming once again. Look how happy you are. You are watching the shadow play so intently. I guess you've got enchanted by the shadow play.

Daniel: Exactly. The shadow play is vivid and also very interesting. The *Wanwan* singing style makes it more appealing.

Han Jia: It seems Daniel has a great interest in the shadow play.

Daniel: Of course. I am very interested in folk arts.

Han Jia: There are various forms of folk arts in Xi'an.

Daniel: What are they?

Han Jia: Such as paper cutting, Shaanxi Opera and the shadow play.

秦腔戏台前

大　牛：这不是秦腔嘛。

韩　佳：对，今年春节的时候，你不是还学过两句嘛？

大　牛：对，我记得。什么"祖籍陕西"。

韩　佳：吼得还不错！

Daniel: Yes, this is Shaanxi Opera.

Han Jia: Right. During the Spring Festival of this year, I remember you learned a few sentences sung in Shaanxi Opera.

Daniel: Yes, I did. The lyrics sound like: "My hometown is Shaanxi..."

Han Jia: You roared pretty well.

西安户县农民画家家中

韩　佳：大牛，你看，这些就是西安户县农民画。

大　牛：真是五彩缤纷！你看，画里的人看上去都是喜气洋洋的，热闹非凡。

韩　佳：对啊，这些农民画色彩非常鲜艳，看上去呢很活泼。⑤

Nóngmín huàr sècǎi fēicháng xiānyàn, kàn shangqu hěn huópo.
农民　画儿 色彩　非常　鲜艳，看　上去　很　活泼。

Peasant paintings are quite colorful and very vivid.

韩　佳：画的都是田园风光和农村生活。这可都是农民画家画的！

大　牛：那你倒是给我们介绍一位啊！

韩　佳：没问题。有请潘晓玲女士，潘女士您好。

嘉　宾：您好。

大　牛：看了您的画我真是特别喜欢，您能不能也教教我？

嘉　宾：可以。我看你很有灵气，我可以收下你这个徒弟。

大　牛：太好了！韩佳，你就看我的吧。

韩　佳：我们去看看大牛能画出什么来。

Han Jia: Daniel, look. These are pictures drawn by farmers of Huxian County of Xi'an.

Daniel: They are so colorful. You see all the characters in the pictures are happy and cheerful, showing a lively and exciting atmosphere.

Han Jia: Yeah, these farmer paintings are quite colorful and very vivid. They all feature rural landscape or country life. These are all works by farmer painters.

Daniel: Why don't you introduce one of them to us?

Han Jia: No problem. Now I have the honor to present Ms. Pan Xiaoling. Good to see you, Ms. Pan.

Ms. Pan: Good to see you.

Daniel: Seeing your paintings, I extremely like them. Could you teach me how to paint?

Ms. Pan: Sure. I can see you are quite smart, so I accept you as my apprentice.

Daniel: Great! Han Jia, you just wait and see.

Han Jia: Let's see what Daniel has painted so far?

作画过程中

嘉　宾：可以了。画得真不错！

大　牛：谢谢，谢谢。

嘉　宾：这个鸡画得真有气质。

韩　佳：大牛，画得怎么样啊？

大　牛：你看呢？

韩　佳：第一次画就能画成这样啊，真挺不错的。

大　牛：这叫名师出高徒，谢谢潘老师。

嘉　宾：不客气。

大　牛：韩佳，刚才潘老师告诉我这农民画里有不少绘画技法呢。

韩　佳：哦，都有哪些啊？

大　牛：有水彩、油画、版画、剪纸，要想画得好，那得花不少时间呢。⑥

韩　佳：那你就要花时间好好练习，厚积薄发。

大　牛：什么叫"厚积薄发"呀？

韩　佳："厚积薄发"中的"厚"是指注重，"薄"是指不注重，"厚积薄发"这个成语是指要注重多积累，不要急于出成绩。⑦

大　牛："厚积薄发"这个成语是指要注重多积累，不要急于出成绩。……可是韩佳，有没有什么更快点儿的办法？

韩　佳：如果想把画儿画好啊，你就得花时间去练习。

Rúguǒ xiǎng bǎ huàr huàhǎo, nǐ jiù děi huā shíjiān qù liànxí.
如果　想　把　画儿　画好，你　就　得　花　时间　去　练习。

If you want to paint great pictures, you need to take time to practice.

韩　佳：你看，潘女士不也那么做嘛。

大　牛：等我练好了，头发都白了！

Ms. Pan: Not bad. A nice picture!

Daniel: Thanks, thanks of it.

Ms. Pan: This rooster you are drawing is quite vivid.

Han Jia: Daniel, how's your painting class going?

Daniel: What do you think of it?

Han Jia: You could do so well in your first painting class. Nice job indeed.

Daniel: An accomplished teacher has skilled students. Thank you, Ms. Pan.

Ms. Pan: You are welcome.

Daniel: Han Jian, Ms. Pan said to me just now that there are many kinds of farmers' pictures.

Han Jia: Oh, what are they?

Daniel: Watercolors, oils, block prints and paper-cuts. If you want to paint really well, you have to spend a lot of time in practicing.

Han Jia: Then, you must spend a lot of time in practicing. "Hou ji bo fa" (practice makes perfection).

Daniel: What is "hou ji bo fa"?

Han Jia: "Hou" in "hou ji bo fa" means "to emphasize". "Bo" means "to ignore or overlook". The idiom "hou ji bo fa" means "to pay attention to learning and practice and not to be too anxious about achievement".

Daniel: "Hou ji bo fa" is a Chinese idiom which means you should be patient in accumulating skills and you shouldn't be too eager to achieve results. ... But, Han Jia, is there a method to acquire the skills faster?

Han Jia: If you want to paint really well, you have to spend time in practicing. Ms. Pan learned her skills also this way.

Daniel: When I am perfect, my hair would've turned grey.

众多画作前

韩　佳：大牛，亏你还说喜欢民间艺术呢！⑧

大　牛：我喜欢欣赏嘛！你看，这儿有这么多艺术品，没人欣赏多可
　　　　惜啊！

韩　佳：这就不用你操心了，西安户县的农民画非常有名，欣赏它的
　　　　人非常多。你啊，就不要再找借口了，赶紧练画儿去。

Han Jia: Daniel, as a folk art lover, you ought not to say so!

Daniel: I love appreciating arts. You see, with so many works of art here, it would be a shame if there were no one to appreciate them.

Han Jia: There is no need to worry about that. The farmers' pictures of Huxian are well known and there are lots of people who appreciate them. You'd better seek no excuse. Go to practice your painting skills.

生词 Words and Expressions

1. 风味　（名）　fēngwèi　special flavor；local color
2. 正宗　（形）　zhèngzōng　genuine
3. 韵味　（名）　yùnwèi　lingering charm；lasting appeal
4. 民间　（名）　mínjiān　folk
5. 祖籍　（名）　zǔjí　original family home；ancestral home
6. 五彩缤纷　　wǔ cǎi bīnfēn　colorful；blazing with color
7. 喜气洋洋　　xǐqì yángyáng　to be full of joy；to be jubilant
8. 非凡　（形）　fēifán　outstanding；extraordinary；uncommon
9. 绘画　（名）　huìhuà　drawing；painting
10. 注重　（动）　zhùzhòng　to lay stress on；to pay attention to

注释 Notes

1. 关中

地区名，指陕西渭河流域一带。

"关中" means the area in the Weihe River basin of Central Shaanxi Plain.

2. 看把你美的。

"美"，形容词，这里指"得意"。"看把你美的"意思是说某人太得意了。用于口语。

The adjective "美" here means "得意". And "看把你美的" means that somebody is too pleased with himself. It is used in the colloquial expression.

例如：这次考试他考了个满分，美的不得了。

3. 是不是喜欢上皮影戏了呀?

"上"这里用在动词后表示动作有了结果并兼有达到某种目的的意思。

"上" is used here after the verb to indicate that the action has got its result and attained some goal at the same time.

例如：这次我们可吃上羊肉泡馍了。

4. 秦腔

一种地方戏曲剧种，流行于西北各省，也叫陕西梆子。

Shaanxi Opera, also known as Shaanxi *Bangzi*, is a local opera popular in the northwestern provinces of China.

5. **看上去**很活泼。

"看上去"，"上去"是动词"看"的补语，"看上去"表示从外表估计、打量。

The structure "看上去", in which "上去" is the complement of the verb "看", means judging from the appearance.

例如：他真年轻，看上去不过二十来岁。

6. **要**想画得好，那得花不少时间呢。

这里"要"是连词，表示假设，"要是"的意思，用于口语。

The colloquial expression "要", a conjunction denoting assumption here, means "要是".

例如：明天你要能来，我们就一起去登长城。

7. 不要急**于**出成绩。

"于"，介词，用于书面语。在形容词后表示方面、原因或目的。

The preposition "于" is used after an adjective in the written language to denote aspects, reasons or goals.

例如：他最近一直忙于论文写作。

8. **亏**你还说喜欢民间艺术呢！

"亏"，动词，表示不怕难为情，用于讥讽。

The verb "亏", meaning "in spite of embarrassment", is used to show sarcasm.

例如：亏你还是个大学生，一点儿礼貌都不懂。

替换练习 Substitution Drills

1. 我　　　　对　　　民间艺术　　　非常　　　感兴趣。
　　他　　　　　　　中国书法　　　　　　　喜欢
　　老张　　　　　　京剧　　　　　　　　　热爱
　　小王　　　　　　故乡　　　　　　　　　有感情

2. 农民画儿　　色彩　非常　鲜艳，看上去很　活泼。
　　　　　　　笔法　　　　简练　　　　　　明快
　　　　　　　技法　　　　细腻　　　　　　雅静
　　　　　　　构思　　　　巧妙　　　　　　有灵气

3. 如果想把　画儿　　画　　好，你就得花时间去练习。
　　　　　　汉语　　学
　　　　　　汉字　　写
　　　　　　钢琴　　弹

会话 Conversation

完成下列会话 Complete the following dialogues
（如括号里有词语或提示，请按要求做 Use words or expressions given in the brackets)

A：那个女孩是谁？长得真漂亮！
B：＿＿＿＿＿＿＿＿＿＿＿＿＿＿＿。（上）
A：是喜欢。她有多大了？
B：＿＿＿＿＿＿＿＿＿＿＿＿＿＿＿。（看上去）

A：昨天的运动会我拿了一个冠军，棒不棒？
B：＿＿＿＿＿＿＿＿＿＿＿＿＿＿＿。（美）
A：这是我每天坚持锻炼的结果。你怎么没参加运动会？
B：＿＿＿＿＿＿＿＿＿＿＿＿＿＿＿。

西安【第十一集】

韩　佳：来到西安市中心，您肯定会被我们身后的这座建筑所吸引。

大　牛：没错，它好像一座城门一样。你听！

韩　佳：这不是城门，这是西安的钟楼。每天早晨呢，都会从这里传
　　　　出报时的钟声。

大　牛：今天我们也去看看。

大　牛：我觉得在市中心修建这样一座仿古钟楼显得特别别致。

韩　佳：它可不是仿古建筑啊！西安钟楼本身就是一座古建筑，距今
　　　　已经有600多年的历史了。

大　牛：原来是这样，可是它好像没有什么损坏嘛。

韩　佳：是啊，西安钟楼保存得十分完整。

Xī'ān　Zhōnglóu　bǎocún　de　shífēn　wánzhěng.

西安　钟楼　保存　得　十分　完整。

Xi'an's Bell Tower has been kept in perfect condition.

146

Han Jia: Now we are in the center of Xi'an. I'm sure you are fascinated by the building behind us.

Daniel: Yes. It looks like a city gate. Listen.

Han Jia: This is not a city gate. It is Xi'an's Bell Tower. Every morning, people hear the strike of the hour coming from the tower.

Daniel: Today, we'll have a visit to the Bell Tower.

Daniel: I think building a bell tower of ancient-style in the center of the city was a unique idea.

Han Jia: But this is no pseudo-ancient structure. The Bell Tower is an ancient structure. It's already more than 600 years old.

Daniel: Oh, I see. But I see little damage in the building.

Han Jia: Yeah. Xi'an's Bell Tower has been kept in perfect condition.

钟楼上，大钟前

大　牛：十点喽！

韩　佳：接着敲啊，大牛。

大　牛：没错啊，十点敲十下嘛。

韩　佳：你应该敲一百零八下。

大　牛：要敲那么多下？

韩　佳：中国古代把一天分为十二个时辰，一个时辰相当于两个小
　　　　时，每个时辰都要报一次时，每次要敲一百零八下。

大　牛：啊，还有这么多讲究？你不说我还真不知道！好像从这里
　　　　也能看到西安的城门。

韩　佳：我们到那边去看看。

Daniel: It's ten o'clock.

Han Jia: Go on striking, Daniel.

Daniel: No, ten strikes for ten o'clock.

Han Jia: You should have struck 108 times.

Daniel: Why that many?

Han Jia: In ancient China, a day was divided into 12 time units, known as "shichen". One "shichen" is equal to two hours. The bell was sounded on every "shichen". And for each "shichen", the bell should be sounded 108 times.

Daniel: Oh, there is so much to know about it. I wouldn't know it if you didn't tell me. It seems we can see the city gates from here.

Han Jia: Let's go over there to take a look.

钟楼上

大　牛：在这儿也能看见城门。

韩　佳：站在西安钟楼上啊，东南西北四座城门都能看见。

大　牛：而且都是正对着的，^①你看，一条笔直的路直通到城门那边。

　　　　韩佳，你看，那边好像还有一座钟楼。

韩　佳：那是鼓楼，和钟楼相对应。中国有一种说法叫"晨钟暮鼓"。

Daniel: We can also see the city gates from here.

Han Jia: Standing on the Xi'an Bell Tower, we can see the north, south, east and west city gates.

Daniel: And the tower is directly facing them. You see four straight streets leading to the gates. Han Jia, look. There seems to be another bell tower over there.

Han Jia: That's the Drum Tower, facing the Bell Tower. There is a saying in China: "People hear the bell in the morning and the drum in the evening."

大　牛：我听说"晨钟暮鼓"指的是寺庙里早上敲钟、傍晚击鼓。

韩　佳：的确是这样，不过城市里的"晨钟暮鼓"跟寺庙里还是有区别的。

大　牛：哦，有什么区别？

韩　佳：古代城市报时是从黄昏开始的，先击鼓一百零八下，然后敲钟一百零八下，每隔两个小时报时一次。

大　牛：看来古代报时的方式和现在完全不一样。

Gǔdài bào shí de fāngfǎ hé xiànzài wánquán bù yíyàng.
古代 报 时 的 方法 和 现在 　完全 　不一样。

Ancient time keeping methods were totally different from those in use today.

大　牛：韩佳，你看，那边的人在干吗呢？

韩　佳：那是古代报时表演要开始了，正好我们可以看看古代人是怎么报时的。[②]

大　牛：好。

Daniel: I was told "chen zhong mu gu" refers to the practice in the temple of striking the bell in the morning and the drum in the evening.

Han Jia: That's exactly true. But "chen zhong mu gu" in cities was different from that of temples.

Daniel: How different?

Han Jia: In ancient cities, the practice to give the time began after sunset with 108 strikes of the bell first, followed by 108 drumbeats, with an interval of every two hours.

Daniel: The way to give the time in ancient times was totally different from that in use today. Han Jia, look, what are they doing over there?

Han Jia: The performance of ancient times to strike the hour has started. Let's go over and see how ancient people gave the time.

Daniel: Good.

大鼓前

大　牛：看起来真威风！我也来试试。中午十二点喽，该吃羊肉泡馍喽！
韩　佳：大牛，你这是在干吗呀？
大　牛：我这不是在报时嘛。
韩　佳：这哪是报时啊？③ 这叫"定更"。"定更"就是在鼓楼这边敲
　　　　响鼓声通知钟楼，钟楼那边就会敲响钟声，通知全城的人
　　　　现在的确切时间，这就叫"鼓楼定更，钟楼报时"。

Gǔlóu dìng gēng, Zhōnglóu bào shí.
鼓楼 定 更， 钟楼 报 时。

**The Drum Tower sounded every two hours at night while the
Bell Tower chimed every hour.**

大　牛：怎么这么讲究呢？
韩　佳：在没有钟表的时候啊，报时是不能随便的，这钟鼓楼的钟鼓
　　　　声呢就是全城的基准时间。这钟鼓楼还可以用来报警呢。
大　牛：三个字——了不起。④

鼓楼上

大　牛：看来钟鼓楼起的作用还真不小。
韩　佳：要不然怎么会把它们建在城市的中心呢。
大　牛：我觉得还是现在方便，只要一抬手……没有了。⑤

154

Daniel: Very impressive! Let me have a try. It's 12, lunchtime. We'd better eat "yangrou pao mo"(pita bread soaked in lamb soup).

Han Jia: Daniel, what are you doing?

Daniel: I am trying to give the time.

Han Jia: You were not giving the time. It's called "ding geng" (determining the time). "Ding geng" was an old practice of beating the drum to inform the Bell Tower that it was time to strike the bell, telling people of the whole city what time it was exactly. So the Drum Tower determined the time while the Bell Tower gave the time.

Daniel: Oh, there is so much to know about it.

Han Jia: When there were no clocks and wrist watches, it wasn't a trivial matter to tell the time. So the Bell Tower and the Drum Tower actually provided the standard time for the city. Besides, they could also be used to give an alarm.

Daniel: They were really important.

Daniel: These towers did play a very important role.

Han Jia: Han Jia: That's why they were built in the center of the city.

Daniel: I think it's a lot easier to tell the time now. With the lift of your hand…

生词 Words and Expressions

1. 报时　（动）　bào shí　to give the correct time
2. 仿古　（动）　fǎnggǔ　to archaize；to be in the style of the ancients
3. 别致　（形）　biézhì　unique；unconventional
4. 损坏　（动）　sǔnhuài　to damage；to spoil
5. 笔直　（形）　bǐzhí　perfectly straight；straight as a ramrod
6. 对应　（动、形）　duìyìng　to correspond with；corresponding
7. 黄昏　（名）　huánghūn　dusk；twilight
8. 报警　（动）　bào jǐng　to report to the police；to give an alarm

注释 Notes

1. **而且都是正对着的。**

　　"正"，副词，表示加强肯定的语气。
　　The adverb "正" is used to intensify the tone of affirmation.
　　例如：这本书正是我要买的。

2. **正好我们可以看看古代人是怎样报时的。**

　　"正好"，副词，这里指时间不前不后，"恰好"的意思。
　　The adverb "正好" means "just in time；as it happens".
　　例如：他是十二月二十五日出生的，那一天正好是圣诞节。

3. **这哪是报时啊？**

　　"哪"，副词，用于反问，表示否定。
　　The adverb "哪" is used in a rhetorical question to denote negation.
　　例如：哪有那么贵的自行车？

4. **三个字——了不起。**

　　"了不起"，意思是"突出，超过一般"。
　　"了不起" means "突出，超过一般" (outstanding，extraordinary).
　　例如：他真了不起，一个人能干几个人的活。

5. **只要一抬手……没有了。**

"只要"，连词，用在条件复句中，后面有副词"就"呼应，"只要"提出所需要的条件，"就"引出有了上述的条件就能产生的结果。

The conjunction "只要", collocating with the adverb "就", is used in a conditional complex sentence, in which "只要" introduces the necessary condition and "就" introduces the result from the afore-mentioned condition.

例如：只要你刻苦努力，就一定能学好。

替换练习 Substitution Drills

1. 西安钟楼　　保存　　得十分　　完整。
　　北海白塔　　修复　　　　　　漂亮
　　圆明园遗址　破坏　　　　　　严重
　　三峡水坝　　修建　　　　　　壮观

2. 古代　报时　的方法和　现在　完全不一样。
　　西医　治病　　　　　　中医
　　小张　学习　　　　　　小王
　　阿里　读书　　　　　　别人

会话 Conversation

完成下列会话 Complete the following dialogues
（如括号里有词语或提示，请按要求做 Use words or expressions given in the brackets）

A：这是鼓楼吗？
B：_____。（哪）
A：鼓楼在什么地方？
B：_____。

A：你英语说得真好，是怎么学的？
B：_____。（只要）
A：你妈妈一定为你感到骄傲吧！
B：_____。（了不起）

西安

【第十二集】

半坡遗址博物馆大门外

大　牛：大家都知道西安是中华民族重要的发源地，它的历史可以追溯到远古时代。

韩　佳：没错儿，我们今天要去西安的半坡遗址，看看 6000 多年前的人们是怎么生活的。

Daniel: As we all know, Xi'an was one of the cradles of the Chinese nation. Its history dates back to remote ages.

Han Jia: Exactly. Today we're going to visit the Banpo Ruins of Xi'an to see how people lived some 6,000 years ago.

第一展室内

韩　佳：大牛，你看。

大　牛：这里陈列的不都是一些石头吗？

韩　佳：应该说是石器。你看，有石斧、石锄、石铲等等，这就说明
　　　　啊在远古时代就有人类在这里繁衍生息了。

Zài yuǎngǔ shídài, jiù yǒu rénlèi zài zhèli fányǎn shēngxī.
在　远古　时代，就　有　人类　在　这里　繁衍　生息。

There has been human habitation here since prehistoric times.

大　牛：什么叫"繁衍生息"啊？

韩　佳："繁衍"啊，就是指逐渐增多，"生息"就是指生存、生活。

大　牛：哦，明白了。"繁衍生息"就是逐步增多的意思。……

韩　佳：大牛，你再来看看这个。

大　牛：这是做什么用的？

韩　佳：这是用来制作石器的，当时的人们就是把石头放在这上面磨
　　　　成各种各样的工具。

大　牛：那当时的人们是靠什么生活的呢？

韩　佳：靠农业、捕鱼、狩猎等等。你看！

大　牛：啊，这是什么？是用来玩的吗？

韩　佳：你就知道玩！①这是用来狩猎的武器。

大　牛：武器？看不出来应该怎么使用。

韩　佳：在狩猎的时候啊，人们把石球拴在绳子上然后再抛出去，这
　　　　样就可以缠住要逃跑的动物了。

大　牛：哦，我明白了，好像现在也能看到这种狩猎方法。

韩　佳：一些原始地区还有人这样做。

大　牛：那6000多年前的人们所有的工具都是石头做的吗？

韩　佳：那倒不是，当时的人啊，还会制作陶器呢。

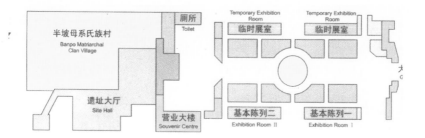

Han Jia: Daniel, look.

Daniel: Aren't they some stones on display?

Han Jia: They are all stone tools on display, such as stone axes, stone hoes and stone spades. They show that there has been human habitation here since prehistoric times.

Daniel: What is "fanyan shengxi"?

Han Jia: "Fanyan" means "to multiply". "Shengxi" means "to survive and live".

Daniel: Oh, I see. "Fanyan shengxi" means "to live and procreate". ...

Han Jia: Look at this, Daniel.

Daniel: What was it used for?

Han Jia: It was used to make stone tools. Ancient people rubbed or polished stones on it to make various kinds of tools.

Daniel: How did ancient people make a living?

Han Jia: They lived by growing crops, fishing and hunting. Look.

Daniel: Eh, what's this? Was it something for fun?

Han Jia: You are only concerned about fun. This was a weapon for hunting.

Daniel: A weapon? I don't know how to use it.

Han Jia: When hunting, the hunter would tie the stone ball to the end of a rope and throw it out to trap an escaping animal.

Daniel: Oh, I see. It seems this hunting method is still in use…

Han Jia: …in some primitive regions.

Daniel: Were all the tools made of stone 6,000 years ago?

Han Jia: Not exactly. People then also made pottery vessels.

韩 佳：大牛，你看这陶盆。

大 牛：这上面画的是什么？既像人脸，又像几条鱼。

韩 佳：这是人面鱼纹，这就说明当时的半坡人对鱼有着特殊的感
情，有人推测这可能是半坡氏族崇奉的图腾。

大 牛：还挺有艺术想象力的嘛！这件陶器做得也不错。

韩 佳：是啊，半坡人熟练地掌握了制作陶器的工艺。

Bànpōrén shúliàn de zhǎngwòle zhìzuò táoqì de gōngyì.
半坡人 熟练 地 掌握了 制作 陶器 的 工艺。

The ancients at Banpo had already mastered the skills
necessary to produce pottery.

Han Jia: Daniel, look at this pottery basin.

Daniel: What's the pattern painted on it? It looks like both a human face and a couple of fish.

Han Jia: It's called the human face and fish pattern. This shows that Banpo primitives had special feelings for fish. Some believed that fish was the totem of Banpo primitives.

Daniel: It does show some artistic imagination. And this is also a finely crafted vessel.

Han Jia: Yes. The ancients at Banpo had already mastered the skills necessary to produce pottery.

韩 佳：看。

大 牛：这又是用来做什么的呀？

韩 佳：这是甑，是用来蒸食物的。

大 牛：那个时候已经学会用水蒸气了啊！那个时候的人不一直什么"毛饮血"的吗？

韩 佳：你是想说"茹毛饮血"？

大 牛：对。

韩 佳：那你知道"茹"是什么意思吗？

大 牛：既然"饮"是喝的意思，那"茹"应该是吃的意思吧。②

韩 佳：嗯，真聪明！"茹"就是吃的意思，"茹毛饮血"就是指把禽兽连毛带血一块儿吞下去，③ 这个词语是用来形容不会用火的原始时代。

大 牛：可这半坡人不但会用火，而且还会利用水蒸气，④ 很聪明！

韩 佳：是啊，这可是人类历史上最早利用水蒸气的范例，这半坡人的智慧可真不能小觑啊。

大 牛：啊？"小区"？

韩 佳："小觑"。"小觑"呢，就是指小看、低估的意思。

大 牛：我明白了。"小觑"，"小"读三声，"觑"读四声，是低估的意思。……古代人的智慧的确不能低估。

Gǔdàirén de zhìhuì díquè bù néng dīgū.
古代人 的 智慧 的确 不 能 低估。

We mustn't underestimate the wisdom of ancient people.

Han Jia: Look.

Daniel: What was this used for?

Han Jia: This is a "zeng" , an earthen utensil for steaming food.

Daniel: So by that time, people had already learned the use of steam. At that time, did people simply "what mao yin xue"?

Han Jia: Did you mean "ru mao yin xue" (to eat raw flesh with fur and blood)?

Daniel: Oh, yeah.

Han Jia: Do you know what "ru" means?

Daniel: Since "yin" means "to drink", "ru" must mean "to eat".

Han Jia: Yes, you are smart. "Ru" means "to eat". "Ru mao yin xue" means "to devour raw animal flesh with both fur and blood". This phrase is used to refer to the primitive times when people didn't know how to make use of fire.

Daniel: I think Banpo people knew not only how to make use of fire, but also how to make use of steam. They were very clever.

Han Jia: Yes. This was the earliest instance of making use of steam in human history. The wisdom of Banpo people shouldn't be underestimated.

Daniel: What? "Xiaoqu" (a little area)?

Han Jia: "Xiaoqu". "Xiaoqu" means "to overlook or underestimate".

Daniel: Oh, I see. "Xiaoqu", third tone, fourth tone, means "to underestimate". ... We mustn't underestimate the wisdom of ancient people.

大　牛：欢迎来到半坡人的家！

韩　佳：大牛，你这是干吗啊？

大　牛：我这不是要体验一下6000年前人们的生活嘛？⑤ 欢迎来到半坡人的家！

韩　佳：你怎么成"半坡人"了啊？ 再说这房子也太黑了吧，怎么住啊？

大　牛：这你就不懂了吧，在6000年前，这种房子是最高级的了，你想住还住不了呢！

韩　佳：瞧把他美的，不管他。

Daniel: Welcome to the home of Banpo people!

Han Jia: Daniel, what are you doing here?

Daniel: I just want to learn the way of life 6,000 years ago. Welcome to the home of Banpo people!

Han Jia: How could you have become a Banpo man? Besides, it's a bit too dim in the house. How could you live here?

Daniel: You don't understand. 6,000 years ago, this would be the best house. You could hardly get one even if you really wanted one.

Han Jia: Look how smug he is. Leave him alone.

生词 Words and Expressions

1. 追溯	（动）	zhuīsù	to trace back to；to date from
2. 狩猎	（动）	shòuliè	to hunt
3. 抛	（动）	pāo	to throw；to toss；to fling
4. 原始	（形）	yuánshǐ	primeval；primitive
5. 氏族	（名）	shìzú	clan
6. 崇奉	（动）	chóngfèng	to believe in；to worship
7. 图腾	（名）	túténg	totem
8. 范例	（名）	fànlì	example；model
9. 智慧	（名）	zhìhuì	wisdom；intelligence
10. 体验	（动）	tǐyàn	to learn through practice；to learn through one's personal experience

注释　Notes

1. 你就知道玩！

"就"，副词，用来限制动作、行为或状态的范围，相当于"只"，这里带有不满的意思。

The adverb "就"，meaning "只" and expressing dissatisfaction here，is used to limit the extent of action，behavior or state.

例如：你就知道花钱，不知道节省。

2. 既然"饮"是喝的意思，那"茹"应该是吃的意思吧。

这是一个因果复句。连词"既然"用于前一分句，提出成为现实的前提，后一分句根据这一前提推出结论。后一分句常有"就""也""还""那"呼应。

This is a cause-effect complex sentence. The conjunction "既然" is used in the first clause，introducing the prerequisite，and the second clause，in which there is "就"，"也"，"还" or "那" collocating with "既然"，is the conclusion from the prerequisite.

例如：你既然身体不舒服，那就不要来了。

3. 把禽兽连毛带血一块儿吞下去。

"连……带……"，这一结构表示包括前后两项或表示两个动作同时发生，不分先后。

The structure " 连 …… 带 ……"indicates that two items or actions happen simultaneously.

例如：他连衣服带洗漱用具都带来了。

孩子连蹦带跳跑了进来。

4．可这半坡人不但会用火，而且还会利用水蒸气。

"不但……而且……"，这是一个递进复句，表示除所说的意思以外，还有更进一层的意思。

The structure "不但……而且……" is used in a progressive complex sentence, denoting in addition to what has been said， there is a further meaning.

例如：他在中国不但学好了汉语，而且还游览了很多地方。

5．我这不是要体验一下6000 年前人们的生活嘛？

"不是……嘛（吗）"是一种反问句式，表示肯定，但它比相应的肯定句式语气要强些。

"不是……嘛（吗）" is a pattern of rhetorical question，denoting affirmation. The tone of the sentence with this structure is stronger than that of the corresponding affirmative sentence.

例如：你不是会说汉语吗？（你会说汉语。）

替换练习 Substitution Drills

1. 在	远古	时代，就有	人类	在这里	繁衍生息。
	秦汉		人		开垦荒地
	隋唐		驻军		守卫边疆
	战国		居民		制造陶器

2. 半坡	人熟练地掌握了	制作	陶器	的	工艺。
中国		加工	玉器		技能
瑞士		制造	钟表		技术
原始		捕捉	野兽		方法

3. 古代	人的	智慧	的确不能	低估。
年轻		才华		小看
老年		作用		轻视
残疾		福利		忽视

会话 Conversation

完成下列会话 Complete the following dialogues
（如括号里有词语或提示，请按要求做 Use words or expressions given in the brackets）

A：你知道古代人是怎么生活的吗？

B：_____。

A：我从博物馆那里了解到古代人生活的一些情况。

B：_____。（既然……那……）

A：明天我们去旅游要带哪些东西呢？

B：_____。（连……带……）

A：去百花山路程远吗？

B：_____。（不但……而且……）

西安【第十三集】

九龙湖岸边

韩　佳：春寒赐浴华清池，温泉水滑洗凝脂。

大　牛：大家好，我是快乐的大牛。

韩　佳：哎，大牛，你这是要干吗去啊？

大　牛：我们今天不是要去泡温泉嘛，我都做好准备了。

韩　佳：我们今天是要去温泉，[①] 但是那温泉啊是只能看，不能泡。

大　牛：啊？只能看，不能泡？这叫什么温泉？我还是回去算了。[②]

韩　佳：哎，等等。这可不是一处普通的温泉，而是一处皇家温泉。

大　牛：是什么温泉？

韩　佳：华清池。

Han Jia: It was early spring. She bathed herself in the Huaqing Pool, which warmed and smoothed the creamy-tinted crystal of her skin.

Daniel: Hello, I am the happy Daniel.

Han Jia: Hey, Daniel, where are you going?

Daniel: Aren't we going to bathe in a hot spring? I have made due preparations.

Han Jia: Yes, we are going to a hot spring. But we can only see it. We can't bathe in it.

Daniel: What? A hot spring only to see and not to use? What kind of hot spring is it? I'd better go back.

Han Jia: Hey, wait a minute. This is no ordinary hot spring. It was an imperial hot spring.

Daniel: What spring?

Han Jia: Huaqing Pool.

场景 Scene 　**海棠汤**

韩　佳：大牛，你看，这就是中国最有名的温泉浴池了。

大　牛：这么小的浴池怎么看也不像皇家用的，你不是在骗我吧？

韩　佳：我怎么会骗你啊？你看看这砌池壁的材料。

大　牛：不就是普通的石头嘛。

韩　佳：这可不是普通的石头，而是上等青石，经过打磨、抛光处理
　　　　之后才形成的。在过去只有皇家才能使用这种材料。③

Zài guòqù, zhǐyǒu huángjiā cái néng shǐyòng zhè zhǒng cáiliào.
在 过去，只有　皇家 才 能　使用　这 种　材料。

**In former times, only royal families were entitled to use
such building materials.**

韩　佳：这华清池可不光因为是皇家浴池才出名的。

大　牛：那还有什么原因？

韩　佳：因为一段爱情故事，唐代的第八位皇帝李隆基和他的妃子杨
　　　　玉环相爱很深。

大　牛：哦，这个故事我知道。唐朝诗人白居易有一首长诗叫《长恨
　　　　歌》，写的就是这个故事。

韩　佳：这就是李隆基送给妃子杨玉环的温泉浴池。

大　牛：我还以为这是诗人自己想象出来的，没想到还真有这么回事。④

韩　佳：我再带你去看看李隆基自己沐浴的场所。

大　牛：走。

Han Jia: Daniel, look, this is China's most famous hot spring pool, the Huaqing Pool.

Daniel: It is too small to be an imperial pool. Are you fooling me?

Han Jia: How can I fool you? Look at the materials used for building the pool.

Daniel: They are just ordinary stones.

Han Jia: They are not ordinary stones. They are all first-rate blue stones, which were all finely polished before being laid here. In former times, only royal families were entitled to use such materials.

Han Jia: The Huaqing Pool became famous not just because it was an imperial bathing pool.

Daniel: Any other reasons?

Han Jia: Also because of the love story of the Tang Dynasty's eighth Emperor Li Longji and his concubine Yang Yuhuan.

Daniel: Oh, I know this story. Bai Juyi, a poet in the Tang Dynasty, wrote a poem, "A Song of Unending Sorrow" about this story.

Han Jia: This is the hot spring bathing pool Li Longji gave to his concubine Yang Yuhuan.

Daniel: I thought the whole affair was an imagination of the poet. I didn't expect it to be true.

Han Jia: Let me take you to see Li Longji's personal bathing pool.

Daniel: Let's go.

莲花汤

大　牛：果然是皇帝李隆基自己用的浴池，就是大。⑤

韩　佳：是啊，这浴池的容水量是贵妃池的六倍，叫莲花汤。浴池的
　　　　形状像一朵莲花。

Yùchí de xíngzhuàng xiàng yì duǒ liánhuā.
浴池 的 　形状　 像 一 朵 莲花。

The pool is in the shape of a lotus flower.

大　牛：韩佳，这"汤"不就是 soup 吗，是喝的。怎么又成浴池了？

韩　佳："汤"最基本的含义呢是热水，后来人们用"汤"来专指温泉。

大　牛：哦，明白了。"汤"，读一声，不光指喝的汤，最基本的含义
　　　　是热水，后来专指温泉。……

韩　佳：现在知道了吧？要是出去看到哪块招牌上面写着"汤池"，
　　　　那就说明是一个热水浴池，⑥ 而不是指餐馆。

大　牛：这回记住了。

Daniel: Indeed, Emperor Li Longji's pool is much bigger.

Han Jia: Yeah. The pool can contain six times as much water as his favorite concubine's. It's called the Lianhuatang Pool. The pool is in the shape of a lotus flower.

Daniel: Han Jia, "tang", or soup, is a kind of food to eat. How come it becomes a bathing pool?

Han Jia: "Tang" originally meant hot water. Later, people began to use the word to refer to a hot spring.

Daniel: Oh, I see. "Tang", first tone, doesn't just mean soup. Its basic meaning was hot water, but later it also acquired the meaning "hot spring". ...

Han Jia: Now you understand? If you go out and see a signboard written with "tangchi" , you should see it as a health spa. It does not refer to a restaurant.

Daniel: I'll remember it.

星辰汤

大　牛：这个浴池简单多了，不用说了这是给仆人用的吧。

韩　佳：猜错了吧，这也是皇帝自己用的，而且是专供唐太宗一个人用的。

大　牛：看着不像嘛，他是不是很节俭啊？

韩　佳：才不是呢！它看着简单，其实它是离水源最近、水流量最大的浴池，在这里沐浴可以体会到冲浪浴的乐趣。

大　牛：看来不能光从表面看问题。俗话说得好："包子好吃，不在褶儿上。"

韩　佳：哟，你还挺幽默！的确，真正的价值光从外表上是看不出来的。

Zhēnzhèng de jiàzhí guāng cóng wàibiǎo shang shì kàn bu chūlái de.
真正 的价值 光 从 外表 上 是 看不出来 的。

It's impossible to determine its real value simply from its appearance.

大　牛：哎，韩佳，我倒是要问问你这华清池温泉到底好在什么地方，引得皇帝选择这里沐浴呢？

韩　佳：那就得从温泉本身说起了。

Daniel: This bath tub is much simpler. Needless to say, it was for the servants.

Han Jia: No, your guess is wrong. It was also for the emperor, and only for Emperor Tang Taizong.

Daniel: It doesn't look like a pool for the emperor. Was he very frugal?

Han Jia: Absolutely not. Though seemingly simple, it is the closest one to the source of the spring and one could get the fastest flow of water. The bather might have had the feel of a surf bath.

Daniel: It seems we mustn't look at things superficially. As the saying goes: "*Baozi* is delicious not because of its wrinkles."

Han Jia: Hey, you are so humorous. Yes, it's impossible to determine its real value simply from its appearance.

Daniel: Hey, Han Jia, just tell me why the Huaqing Pool was so good that an emperor of the Tang Dynasty decided to bathe here.

Han Jia: We have to start from the hot spring.

181

韩　佳：这里的温泉水温保持在 43 度，而且流量很大，还有治疗作用，所以人们都说在这里泡完了温泉之后呢，是"冬天走十里路不冷，夏天走十里路不热"。

大　牛：听起来很神奇，就是不知道是不是真的。

韩　佳：那等我先去试试再告诉你吧。

大　牛：啊？你不是说这里是只能看不能泡吗？

韩　佳：那是温泉遗址，在离这里不远处您可以亲自感受一下华清池温泉。

大　牛：你怎么不早说呀？

韩　佳：现在说也不晚啊。

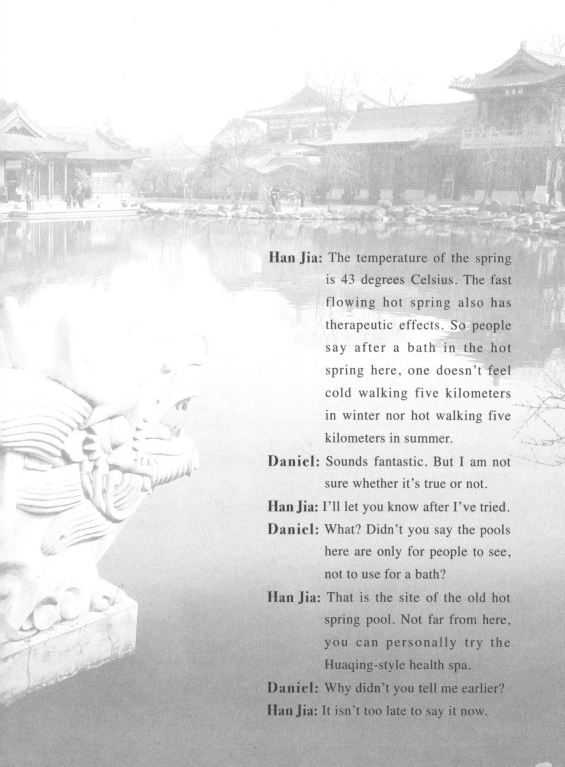

Han Jia: The temperature of the spring is 43 degrees Celsius. The fast flowing hot spring also has therapeutic effects. So people say after a bath in the hot spring here, one doesn't feel cold walking five kilometers in winter nor hot walking five kilometers in summer.

Daniel: Sounds fantastic. But I am not sure whether it's true or not.

Han Jia: I'll let you know after I've tried.

Daniel: What? Didn't you say the pools here are only for people to see, not to use for a bath?

Han Jia: That is the site of the old hot spring pool. Not far from here, you can personally try the Huaqing-style health spa.

Daniel: Why didn't you tell me earlier?

Han Jia: It isn't too late to say it now.

生词 Words and Expressions

1. 泡	（动）	pào	to steep；to soak
2. 温泉	（名）	wēnquán	hot spring
3. 打磨	（动）	dǎmó	to polish；to burnish；to shine
4. 沐浴	（动）	mùyù	to have a bath
5. 莲花	（名）	liánhuā	lotus flower；lotus
6. 节俭	（形）	jiéjiǎn	thrifty；frugal
7. 流量	（名）	liúliàng	flow capacity；discharge
8. 冲浪浴	（名）	chōnglàngyù	surfing bath
9. 褶儿	（名）	zhěr	pleat；crease
10. 治疗	（动）	zhìliáo	to treat；to cure

注释 Notes

1. 我们今天**是**要去温泉。

   "是"在这里表示肯定，有"的确"的意思。

   "是" is used here to denote affirmation，meaning "的确" (indeed，surely).

   例如：我大学毕业后是要考研究生。

2. 我**还是**回去**算了**。

   "还是"，副词，表示经过比较考虑后做出的选择。

   The adverb "还是" is used to express a preference for an alternative out of comparison and consideration.

   例如：北方太冷，还是去南方吧。

   "算了"，作罢，事情到此为止。

   "算了" means "to let it be；let it pass".

   例如：算了，别再说了。

3. 在过去**只有**皇家**才**能使用这种材料。

   "只有……才……"这是一个条件复句结构，连词"只有"指出唯一的条件，副词"才"引出有了上述的条件就会产生的结果。

The structure "只有……才……" is used in a conditional complex sentence, in which the conjunction "只有" introduces the one and only condition, and the adverb "就" introduces the result from the afore-mentioned condition.

例如：只有勤奋努力，才能学到科学知识。

4. 我还**以为**这是诗人自己想象出来的，没想到还真有这么回事。

"以为"，动词，常用来表示作出的判断往往不符合事实，后面用另一个句子指明真相。

The verb "以为" is often used to indicate that one's judgment does not accord with the fact, and the truth is shown clearly in the next clause.

例如：他以为下雨了，其实没有下。

5. **果然**是皇帝李隆基自己用的浴池，就是大。

"果然"，副词，表示事实跟所说的或所预料的情况相符合。

The adverb "果然" is used to indicate that the fact accords with what has been said or expected.

例如：听说杭州西湖的景色很美，到那儿一看果然不错。

6. **要是**出去看到哪块招牌上写着"汤池"，那**就**说明是一个热水浴池。

"要是……(那)就……"，这是一个假设复句，"要是"提出一种假设，"就"引出在这种情况下出现的结果。

The structure "要是……(那)就……" is used in a hypothetical complex sentence, in which "要是" introduces hypothesis, and "就" introduces the result from the afore-mentioned hypothesis.

例如：要是明天下雨我就不去了。

替换练习 Substitution Drills

1. 在过去，只有　　皇家　　才能　　使用　　这种材料。
　　　　　　　　　富人　　　　　　吃得起　山珍海味
　　　　　　　　　贵族　　　　　　修建　　深宅大院
　　　　　　　　　高官　　　　　　住进　　高级宾馆

2. 浴池　　　　的形状像一　　朵　　莲花。
　　体育馆　　　　　　　　　把　　大伞
　　火箭　　　　　　　　　　根　　圆柱体
　　汽车　　　　　　　　　　个　　乌龟壳

3. 真正的　价值　光　从　外表上　是　看不出来　的。
　　　　　知识　只　　　书本上　　　学不到
　　　　　思想　仅　　　发言中　　　摸不透
　　　　　想法　单　　　谈话中　　　搞不清

会话 Conversation

完成下列会话 Complete the following dialogues
（如括号里有词语或提示，请按要求做 Use words or expressions given in the brackets）

A：你看这华清池多么华美啊！
B：＿＿＿＿＿＿＿＿＿＿＿＿＿＿＿＿。（果然）
A：这华清池是名胜古迹，可不能下去泡啊。
B：＿＿＿＿＿＿＿＿＿＿＿＿＿＿＿＿。（算了）

A：你原来想到这里来泡温泉？
B：＿＿＿＿＿＿＿＿＿＿＿＿＿＿＿＿。（以为）
A：你真傻，还想像李隆基那样来泡温泉呢。
B：＿＿＿＿＿＿＿＿＿＿＿＿＿＿＿＿。（要是……就……）

西安

【第十四集】

背景为骊山山峰

韩 佳：说起这西安的风景啊，有个地方可不能错过。

大 牛：哦，是什么地方？

韩 佳：就是这里——林木苍翠、绵延起伏的骊山。

大 牛：你别说，这里的景色真不错！①

韩 佳：那我们今天呢就带大家去饱览一下骊山的美景。

大 牛：走。

Han Jia: Talking about Xi'an's scenic spots, there's a place we mustn't miss.

Daniel: What is it?

Han Jia: It's right here, the undulating Lishan Mountain covered with pine trees.

Daniel: Indeed, the scenery here is excellent.

Han Jia: Today, we are going to take our audience on a tour of the scenic Lishan Mountain.

Daniel: Let's go.

骊山小路上

韩　佳：早在2000多年前啊，就有关于骊山的记载了。②

大　牛：还挺早的嘛。

韩　佳：那当然了，骊山很早以前就是著名的旅游胜地了，一直以来
　　　　骊山的美景吸引了络绎不绝的游人。③

Líshān de měijǐng xīyǐnle luòyì bù jué de yóurén.
骊山 的 美景 吸引了 络绎 不 绝 的 游人。

**The beautiful scenery of Lishan Mountain attracts
a steady stream of visitors.**

大　牛：不断地有游人来，这骊山不就是古今驰名吗？

韩　佳：对啊，"驰名"啊就是指名声传播得很远，是个褒义词。

大　牛："驰名"，都读二声，指名声传播得很远。……我觉得到这里
　　　　登高望远真是心旷神怡。

韩　佳：哎，对了。你知道为什么叫"骊山"吗？

大　牛：这还有为什么，这就像你叫韩佳、我叫大牛一样，不就是个
　　　　名字嘛。

韩　佳：你呀，肯定是不知道。这骊山高大、雄壮，远远看去就像一
　　　　匹黑色的骏马，所以呢，就叫"骊山"。

大　牛：哦，原来"骊山"的"骊"就是一匹黑色的骏马的意思。可
　　　　是你看这里青山绿树，应该是一匹青色的骏马才对啊。

Han Jia: There were written records about the mountain as early as more than 2,000 years ago.

Daniel: It became known a long time ago.

Han Jia: Of course. The Lishan Mountain was already a famous resort a very long time ago. Its beautiful scenery attracts a continuous stream of visitors.

Daniel: Thanks to their visits, the Lishan Mountain has become famous in China.

Han Jia: Oh, "chiming" means "to have one's name spread far and wide". It's a commendatory word.

Daniel: "Chiming", two second tones, means "to be known far and wide". ... Watching the distant views from this high point makes me completely relaxed and joyful.

Han Jia: Yeah. But do you know why it's called Lishan?

Daniel: It doesn't need any reasons, just like why you are called Han Jia and why I am called Daniel. It's just a name.

Han Jia: Hey, I'm sure you don't know. The mountain is high and magnificent. It looks like a dark sturdy horse from a distance. So people called it the Lishan Mountain.

Daniel: Oh, the "li" in "Lishan" actually means a dark sturdy horse. But you see it's a blue mountain with green trees. It should be called a blue sturdy horse.

骊山老母殿内

大　牛：原来这里是一座道观。

韩　佳：那你知道这里供奉的是谁吗？

大　牛：不知道。

韩　佳：就是女娲。

大　牛：就是中国神话中修补天空的那个"女娲"呀？

韩　佳：没错儿，传说她用泥土创造了人类，并且就在骊山上采石补天。④

大　牛：原来"女娲补天"的故事就发生在这里。

韩　佳：真正的女娲有可能是远古时代的一位氏族首领，就住在骊山附近。

大　牛：听你这么一说，我觉得这里挺神奇的。⑤

韩　佳：对啊，这里不但风景壮美，而且传说神奇。

Zhèli　búdàn　fēngjǐng　zhuàngměi,　érqiě　chuánshuō　shénqí.
这里　不但　风景　壮美，　而且　传说　神奇。

It's not only a place of beautiful scenery, but also a place of legendary folk tales.

Daniel: There is a Taoist temple here.

Han Jia: Do you know who is enshrined here?

Daniel: No, I don't.

Han Jia: It's Nüwa.

Daniel: That Nüwa who mended the sky in Chinese mythology?

Han Jia: Exactly. Legend has it that she created humans with mud and mended the sky with stones she got right on the Lishan Mountain.

Daniel: Oh, the story of Nüwa mending the sky took place right here.

Han Jia: The real Nüwa could have been a chief of a primitive tribe residing on the Lishan Mountain.

Daniel: Hearing what you said, I think this place is really mysterious.

Han Jia: Yeah, it's not only a place of beautiful scenery, but also a place of legendary folk tales.

烽火台下

大　牛：哟，这不就是烽火台吗？

韩　佳：对啊，以前每当敌人来犯的时候，就是在这里点起狼烟报信的。

大　牛：古代人真有意思，⑥老喜欢把城墙建在山顶上。

韩　佳：这可不是什么城墙啊。

大　牛：可是你看，这长城上的烽火台就是和城墙连在一起的，这里有烽火台就说明这里有城墙。

韩　佳：不是这样的，这烽火台不一定要跟城墙连在一起。你啊，不要什么事情都想当然。

大　牛：什么叫"想当然"呢？

韩　佳："想当然"就是说凭主观推测认为事情应该或大概是这个样子。

大　牛："想当然"，"想"读三声，"当"读一声，"然"读二声；就是凭主观推测，认为事情应该是这个样子。……

韩　佳：所以啊，你不要想当然地认为烽火台一定要跟城墙连在一起。

大　牛：我明白了，只要是建在高处、便于观察就行了。

韩　佳：对，以前每隔一段距离就会在高处建一座烽火台。不过现在这附近啊只剩下这一座了。

大　牛：那再也看不到"烽火连天"的景象了。

fēnghuǒ　liántiān
烽火　　连天

the flames of war burned high into the sky

韩　佳："烽火连天"是指战争来了，看不见才好呢。来，我们接着往下看。

194

Daniel: Wow, isn't this a watch tower?

Han Jia: Yeah. In the past, whenever invading troops arrived, fire would be lit here to send out smoke signals.

Daniel: Ancient people were really interesting. They always preferred to build their city walls on top of mountains.

Han Jia: But this is not a city wall.

Daniel: But, as you know, the watch towers on the Great Wall were built together with the wall. Since there is a watch tower here, there must be a similar wall around here.

Han Jia: No, it's not the case. A watch tower wasn't built necessarily to link a wall. You mustn't make conclusions on assumptions.

Daniel: What does "xiangdangran" mean?

Han Jia: "Xiangdangran" means "to believe that things are probably so purely based on assumptions".

Daniel: "Xiangdangran", third tone, first tone, second tone, means "to make subjective assumptions". ...

Han Jia: So you mustn't take it for granted that a watch tower must be connected with a wall.

Daniel: Now I am clear. It would be enough as long as it was built on a higher place convenient for watching.

Han Jia: Yes. In the past, watch towers would be built on higher places at certain intervals. But today, there is only one watch tower remaining around here.

Daniel: So it would be impossible to see the scenes of "fenghuo liantian".

Han Jia: "Fenghuo liantian" means the flames of war burned high into the sky. It would be much better not to see those scenes. Let's go on with our tour.

韩　佳：大牛，你看那是什么？

大　牛：那不就是天文台吗？

韩　佳：那你知道它是干什么用的吗？

大　牛：天文台就是观察宇宙用的，还能做什么用呢？

韩　佳：这里啊，是国家授时中心，中国的标准时间呢就是从这里发
　　　　布的。

大　牛：哦，原来北京时间就是在这里定的。

韩　佳：对啊，北京时间可不是在北京发布的。

大　牛：真是不来不知道，什么事都不能想当然。

韩　佳：学得还挺快！

Han Jia: Daniel, what's that?

Daniel: Isn't it an observatory?

Han Jia: Do you know what it's used for?

Daniel: An observatory is for the observation of the universe. For what else would it be used?

Han Jia: This is the National Time Service Center. China's standard time is issued right from here.

Daniel: Oh, the standard Beijing time is actually set here.

Han Jia: Yes. The Beijing time isn't issued from Beijing.

Daniel: I wouldn't know it if I didn't come here. Nothing can be taken for granted.

Han Jia: You are learning very fast.

生词 Words and Expressions

1. 绵延起伏　　　　　miányán qǐfú　　　to be continuous and undulating
2. 络绎不绝　　　　　luòyì bù jué　　　in an endless stream
3. 褒义　　（名）　　bāoyì　　　commendatory sense
4. 心旷神怡　　　　　xīn kuàng shén yí　　relaxed and joyful；carefree and happy
5. 供奉　　（动）　　gòngfèng　　　to make offerings to；to consecrate
6. 首领　　（名）　　shǒulǐng　　　chieftain；leader；head
7. 烽火　　（名）　　fēnghuǒ　　　beacon-fire
8. 狼烟　　（名）　　lángyān　　　the smoke of wolves' dried dung burnt at border posts in ancient China to signal alarm
9. 宇宙　　（名）　　yǔzhòu　　　universe；cosmos

注释 Notes

1. 你别说，这里的景色真不错！

　　"你别说"，口头语，用在句子的开头，加重后面句子的肯定语气。后面句子表示出乎意料。

　　The pet phrase "你别说" is used at the beginning of a sentence to emphasize the affirmative tone of the sentence following it. And the following sentence indicates that something is out of one's expectations.

　　例如：你别说，这种水果还真好吃。

2. 早在 2000 多年前啊，就有关于骊山的记载了。

　　"关于"，介词，表示涉及的事物。
　　The preposition "关于" indicates the thing involved.
　　例如：最近我看了一些关于中国经济改革的书籍。

3. 一直以来骊山的美景吸引了络绎不绝的游人。

　　"以来"，助词，表示从过去某时直到说话时（或特指的某一时间）为止的一段时间。

　　The function word "以来" refers to the period of time from sometime in the past to the moment of speaking （or sometime referred specifically to）.

例如：开学以来我就没有踢过球。

4. **传说她用泥土创造了人类，并且就在骊山上采石补天。**

"并且"，连词，表示更进一层的意思。

The conjunction "并且" is used to indicate a further meaning.

例如：大家要认真学习，并且要长期坚持下去。

5. **听你这么一说，我觉得这里挺神奇的。**

"这么一"，"这么"起加强语气的作用。动词前面加"一"表示经过某一短暂动作就得出某种结果或结论。

In the structure "这么一"，"这么" is used to intensify the tone. Placing "一" before a verb means that once a transitory action is done, some result or conclusion will be achieved.

例如：这么一用力，就把瓶子打开了。

6. **古代人真有意思。**

"有意思"，指有趣味、有情趣，用于口语。

"有意思"，a colloquial expression, means "interesting or enjoyable".

例如：奥运会的吉祥物设计得真有意思。

替换练习 Substitution Drills

1. 骊山	的	美景	吸引了	络绎不绝	的	游人。
动物园		大熊猫		来来往往		参观者
中国		市场		世界各国		商人
哈尔滨		冰雕		全国各地		艺术家

2. 这里	不但	风景壮美，	而且	传说神奇。
		物产丰富		人口众多
		气候宜人		环境优美
		山多地少		缺乏水源

199

3. 烽火　　连天
　　炮火
　　芳草
　　湖水

会话 Conversation

完成下列会话 Complete the following dialogues
（如括号里有词语或提示，请按要求做 Use words or expressions given in the brackets）

A：你看这宫殿修建得多豪华，住起来一定挺舒服的。

B：＿＿＿＿＿＿＿＿＿＿＿＿＿＿＿。（你别说）

A：你知道唐代皇帝李隆基的故事吗？

B：＿＿＿＿＿＿＿＿＿＿＿＿＿＿＿。（这么一说）

A：《长恨歌》这篇诗写的就是李隆基的爱情故事。

B：＿＿＿＿＿＿＿＿＿＿＿＿＿＿＿。（以来）

A：杨贵妃也是中国历史上的一位美女吧？

B：＿＿＿＿＿＿＿＿＿＿＿＿＿＿＿。（之一）

西安
【第十五集】

场景 Scene 大唐芙蓉园内集市

韩 佳：说起这西安小吃啊，那真是让人垂涎欲滴啊。

大 牛：没错儿，有什么凉皮、羊肉泡馍、肉夹馍、葫芦头。

韩 佳：嘿，你还什么都知道！

大 牛：这么有名能不知道吗？只是我一样都没尝过。^①

韩 佳：啊，一样都没尝过啊？没尝过西安小吃啊，就不算来过
西安。^②

Méi chángguo Xī'ān xiǎochī jiù bú suàn láiguo Xī'ān.

没 尝过 西安 小吃 就 不 算 来过 西安。

**If you haven't tasted Xi'an's snacks, you haven't really
been to Xi'an.**

大 牛：要不今天你带我去尝一尝？

韩 佳：好，没问题，今天我们就向着西安小吃出发。

大 牛：走。

202

Han Jia: Talking about Xi'an's snacks, they really make my mouth watering.

Daniel: Exactly. Such as bean jelly, pita bread soaked in mutton soup, pita bread stuffed with meat and tripe soup.

Han Jia: Hey, you know them all.

Daniel: Why, they are all well-known snacks. But only I have never tasted any of them.

Han Jia: Ah, never? If you haven't tasted Xi'an's snacks, you haven't really been to Xi'an.

Daniel: Do you mind taking me to have a taste today?

Han Jia: No problem. Our destination today is the place for Xi'an's snacks.

Daniel: Let's go.

餐厅内

服务员：两位慢用。

韩 佳：谢谢。

服务员：不客气。

大 牛：韩佳。

韩 佳：嗯？

大 牛：你要请我吃烧饼啊？

韩 佳：我要请你吃西安著名的小吃——羊肉泡馍啊。

大 牛：可是我也没见到羊肉啊！

韩 佳：嗨，你别着急。吃羊肉泡馍的第一步啊就是要亲自动手，把馍掰成小块儿，然后再倒入羊汤煮一煮就可以吃了。

大 牛：先把这个馍给吃了，再喝掉羊汤不一样也是泡着吗？

韩 佳：你这是瞎掰。

大 牛：我根本没打算掰。

韩 佳：嗨，我说的"瞎掰"啊并不是指掰这个动作，而是指胡乱地编造一些话。

大 牛："瞎掰"，都读一声，指胡乱地编造一些话。……看来我还是老老实实地掰吧。

Waitress: Help yourselves, please.

Han Jia: Thanks.

Waitress: You are welcome.

Daniel: Han Jia.

Han Jia: Yes?

Daniel: You want to treat me to pita bread?

Han Jia: I want to treat you to the famous Xi'an *yangrou paomo* (pita bread soaked in mutton soup).

Daniel: But I see no lamb here.

Han Jia: Don't worry. The first step to eat *yangrou paomo* is to break off the bread into small pieces with your own hands. Then soak them in boiling mutton soup before you start eating it.

Daniel: But why not eat the bread first and then eat the soup to let it soaked in my stomach?

Han Jia: You are "xiabai" (talking nonsense).

Daniel: I didn't intend to break the bread at all.

Han Jia: The"xiabai" I said doesn't refer to the act of breaking off something with your hands. It means "to fabricate stories or talk nonsense".

Daniel: "Xiabai", two first tones, means "to talk absolute nonsense". ... It seems I should honestly"bai"(to break off) the bread.

 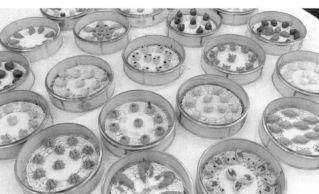

餐厅内

大　牛：嗯，煮好了，我来尝一尝。

韩　佳：怎么样，味道不错吧？

大　牛：都说到了西安不吃羊肉泡馍，就像到了北京不去长城一样，是一种遗憾。

韩　佳：这羊肉泡馍啊是中国有名的小吃。

Yángròu pàomó shì Zhōngguó yǒumíng de xiǎochī.
羊肉　　泡馍　是　中国　　有名　的　小吃。

Yangrou paomo (mutton and bread soup) is a popular snack　in China.

韩　佳：吃过之后呢，唇齿留香、浑身舒畅，保证您啊吃一碗想两碗，吃两碗想三碗。

大　牛：我已经想好了要吃几碗了。

韩　佳：几碗？

大　牛：三碗。

Daniel: Yes,it's well cooked. Let me taste it.

Han Jia: Does it taste good?

Daniel: Not eating *yangrou paomo* in Xi'an, like not visiting the Great Wall in Beijing, would be a big pity.

Han Jia: *Yangrou paomo* is a popular snack in China. After eating it, the pleasant aftertaste will make you feel refreshed. And you will definitely want a second helping and even a third one.

Daniel: I've decided how much I'll eat.

Han Jia: How much?

Daniel: Three helpings.

大　牛：哟，这么多精致的小点心！

韩　佳：这可不是小点心啊，这是西安有名的饺子宴。

大　牛：啊，难道整个一桌宴席都是饺子？那会不会太单调了？

韩　佳：放心吧，这饺子宴啊是一饺一形、百饺百味儿，也就是说每一种饺子都有它独特的形状，③ 也有它独特的味道。

大　牛：嗯，没错。

韩　佳：这是什么味儿的？

大　牛：这是猪肉的。

韩　佳：再尝尝，那个。这个呢……什么味儿？

大　牛：这是鸭肉的。

韩　佳：吃吃这个，这是四喜饺子。

大　牛：海味儿的。嗯，不错！

韩　佳：这儿有不同味道的饺子。

Zhèr　yǒu　bù　tóng　wèidào　de　jiǎozi.
这儿 有 不 同　味道 的 饺子。

There are dumplings of different flavors.

Daniel: Wow, such exquisite tiny dim sums.

Han Jia: But they are not dim sums. This is Xi'an's famous *jiaozi* feast.

Daniel: What, a whole table of *jiaozi*? Wouldn't that be too monotonous?

Han Jia: Take it easy. Each *jiaozi* takes a different shape and tastes different, which means the dumplings are all different both in shape and taste.

Daniel: Yeah, you are right.

Han Jia: What is the filling?

Daniel: It's pork.

Han Jia: Try another one. And this one... What is the filling?

Daniel: Duck.

Han Jia: And try this one. It's the "four-happiness *jiaozi*".

Daniel: It's seafood. Mm, not bad.

Han Jia: There are dumplings of different flavors.

韩　佳：你想不想尝尝锅里的啊？

大　牛：锅里是什么？

韩　佳：打开看看，来。这锅里的叫珍珠饺子，尝尝。

大　牛：还真的像珍珠一样。怎么只有一个啊？

韩　佳：你吃到一个呢，就说明啊，你会"一帆风顺"。怎么样？

大　牛：哎，错了，里面还有一个。

韩　佳：那就说明你会"双喜临门"呗。

大　牛：那我要是吃到十个呢？

韩　佳：十个就是"十全十美"，反正不管你吃到几个，都说明你是
　　　　有福气的。④

大　牛：那我要多吃几个。

Han Jia: Do you want to try those in the pot?

Daniel: What are those in the pot?

Han Jia: Open the lid. Come on. They are called the "pearl *jiaozi*". Taste one.

Daniel: It does look like a pearl. But why only one?

Han Jia: If you happen to have one, it means you will be "yi fan feng shun" (a favorable wind all the way). Not bad?

Daniel: Oh, I am wrong. There is another one here.

Han Jia: That means you'll have double happiness.

Daniel: What if I have ten?

Han Jia: That will be "shi quan shi mei" (perfect in every respect). No matter how many you happen to have, you will always be lucky.

Daniel: Then I'll eat some more.

生词　Words and Expressions

1. 垂涎欲滴　　　　chuí xián yù dī　　one's mouth drools with greed；one's mouth waters

2. 掰　　　（动）　bāi　　　　　　to break off with hands

3. 遗憾　　（形）　yíhàn　　　　　regretful

4. 浑身　　（名）　húnshēn　　　　from head to heel；all over the body

5. 单调　　（形）　dāndiào　　　　monotonous；dull；drab

6. 海味儿　（名）　hǎiwèir　　　　choice seafood

7. 珍珠　　（名）　zhēnzhū　　　　pearl

8. 一帆风顺　　　　yì fān fēng shùn　plain sailing；smooth sailing

9. 双喜临门　　　　shuāng xǐ lín mén　double blessings have descended upon the house

10. 十全十美　　　shí quán shí měi　to be perfect in every way；to be the acme of perfection；to leave nothing to be desired

注释　Notes

1. 只是我一样都没有尝过。

　　"只是"，连词，承接上文，引进对上文的补充说明。

　　The conjunction "只是" continues from the preceding clause and introduces the complementary explanation.

　　例如：对他我不了解，只是见过一次面。

2. 没尝过西安小吃啊，就不算来过西安。

　　"算"，动词，"认做""认为是"的意思。

　　The verb "算" means "认做" or "认为是" (to be considered).

　　例如：他学习很努力，可以算（是）好学生。

3. 也就是说每一种饺子都有它独特的形状。

　　"就"，副词，表示加强肯定。

The adverb "就" is used to emphasize the tone of affirmation.

例如：我家就是住在这个胡同里。

4．反正**不管**你吃到几个，**都**说明你是有福气的。

"不管……都……"，这是一个条件复句，表示在任何条件下结果都是一样。"不管"引出的是条件，"都"引出结果。

The structure "不管 …… 都 ……" is used in a conditional complex sentence, indicating that under whatever conditions, the result will be the same. "不管" introduces the condition, and "都" introduces the result.

例如：不管怎么忙，他每周都要给妈妈写信。

替换练习 Substitution Drills

1. 没	尝	过	西安	小吃	就不算来过	西安。
	吃		北京	烤鸭		北京
	登		中国	长城		中国
	游		杭州	西湖		杭州

2. 羊肉泡馍	是	中国	有名的	小吃。
萨琪玛		北京		点心
五香豆		上海		特产
山竹		泰国		水果

3. 这儿有不同	味道	的	饺子。
	款式		服装
	品牌		电脑
	种类		水稻

会话 Conversation

完成下列会话 Complete the following dialogues
（如括号里有词语或提示，请按要求做 Use words or expressions given in the brackets）

A：你吃过正宗的烤鸭吗？

B：_____。（只是）

A：我今天带你去前门烤鸭店去吃一次地道的烤鸭。

B：_____。（不算）

• •

A：你吃过四川火锅吗？

B：_____。

A：今天我请你吃四川火锅。你说去哪个餐馆好？

B：_____。（不管……都……）

最宜人的季节：

西安四季分明，气候温和。除了较寒冷的冬季外，其他季节都比较适合旅游。

不可错过的景点：

钟楼、鼓楼、大雁塔、小雁塔、明城墙、碑林、陕西历史博物馆、半坡博物馆、秦始皇陵、秦兵马俑、华清池、骊山森林公园、秦岭野生动物园等等。

最舒适的着装：

休闲装

机场（火车站）距市中心路程：

咸阳国际机场位于西安市西北部，距西安市中心约50公里，有机场高速公路连通，1小时可达，西安市区至机场的班车起点在西稍门民航售票处。

富有特色的地方美食：

饺子宴、仿唐宴和牛羊肉泡馍被誉为西安饮食"三绝"。大菜之外，还有各种各样具有地方特色的小吃，腊汁肉夹馍、葫芦头、黄桂稠酒、腊牛羊肉、柿子饼、灌汤包子、面皮等等。

独一无二的特产：

特产：大枣、核桃、火晶柿子、石榴、猕猴桃、黑米、西凤酒、腊牛羊肉、乾县锅盔、西乡牛肉、甘泉豆腐干、陕西板栗等等。

民间工艺品：仿古青铜器、秦俑仿制品、碑林拓片、秦绣、丝绸、工艺瓷器、户县农民画、唐三彩、麦秆画、关中剪纸、凤翔泥塑、藤编、秦腔脸谱、皮影等等。

特别提示：

西安少数民族以回族居多，回族小吃也是西安饮食文化的代表，旅行时一定要尊重民族习惯。

图书在版编目（CIP）数据

快乐中国——学汉语. 西安篇 /《快乐中国——学汉语》栏目组编.
—北京：北京语言大学出版社，2009 重印
ISBN 978 - 7 - 5619 - 1609 - 4

Ⅰ. 快…
Ⅱ. 快…
Ⅲ. 汉语 - 视听教学 - 对外汉语教学 - 教材
Ⅳ. H195.4

中国版本图书馆 CIP 数据核字（2006）第 025871 号

书　　名：快乐中国——学汉语. 西安篇
责任编辑：王　轩　望　震
封面设计：张志伟　贾　英　卜秀敏
责任印制：汪学发

出版发行：北京语言大学出版社
社　　址：北京市海淀区学院路 15 号　邮政编码：100083
网　　址：www.blcup.com
电　　话：发行部　82303650/3591/3651
　　　　　编辑部　82303647
　　　　　读者服务部　82303653/3908
　　　　　网上订购电话　82303668
　　　　　客户服务信箱　service@blcup.net
印　　刷：北京中科印刷有限公司
经　　销：全国新华书店

版　　次：2007 年 7 月第 1 版　2009 年 4 月第 2 次印刷
开　　本：710 毫米×980 毫米　1/16　印张：14
字　　数：199 千字　　印数：4001 - 7000 册
书　　号：ISBN 978 - 7 - 5619 - 1609 - 4/H·06056
定　　价：70.00 元

凡有印装质量问题，本社负责调换。电话：82303590